Water Quality Vital Signs Monitoring Protocol for the Pacific Island Network

Volume 1. Report Narrative

Version 1.0

Natural Resource Report NPS/ PACN/NRR—2011/418

Tahzay Jones, Kimber DeVerse, Gordon Dicus, Danielle McKay, Anne Farahi, Kelly Kozar, and Eric Brown

National Park Service
Pacific Island Inventory and Monitoring Network
Hawaii Volcanoes National Park
PO Box 52
Hawaii National Park, Hawaii 96718
November 2010

U.S. Department of the Interior
National Park Service
Pacific West Regional Office
Oakland, California

June 2011

U.S. Department of the Interior
National Park Service
Natural Resource Stewardship and Science
Fort Collins, Colorado

The National Park Service, Natural Resource Stewardship and Science office in Fort Collins, Colorado publishes a range of reports that address natural resource topics of interest and applicability to a broad audience in the National Park Service and others in natural resource management, including scientists, conservation and environmental constituencies, and the public.

The Natural Resource Report Series is used to disseminate high-priority, current natural resource management information with managerial application. The series targets a general, diverse audience, and may contain NPS policy considerations or address sensitive issues of management applicability.

All manuscripts in the series receive the appropriate level of peer review to ensure that the information is scientifically credible, technically accurate, appropriately written for the intended audience, and designed and published in a professional manner. This report received formal, high-level peer review based on the importance of its content, or its potentially controversial or precedent-setting nature. Peer review was conducted by highly qualified individuals with subject area technical expertise and was overseen by a peer review manager.

Views, statements, findings, conclusions, recommendations, and data in this report do not necessarily reflect views and policies of the National Park Service, U.S. Department of the Interior. Mention of trade names or commercial products does not constitute endorsement or recommendation for use by the U.S. Government.

This report is available from the Pacific Island I&M Network website (http://www.nature.nps.gov/im/units/pacn/) and the Natural Resource Publications Management website (http://www.nature.nps.gov/publications/nrpm/).

Please cite this publication as:

Jones, T., K. DeVerse, G. Dicus, D. McKay, A. Farahi, K. Kozar, and E. Brown. 2011. Water quality vital signs monitoring protocol for the Pacific Island Network:Volume 1; Version 1.0. Natural Resource Report NPS/PACN/NRR—2011/418. National Park Service, Fort Collins, Colorado.

NPS 988/108127, June 2011

Contents

Contents (continued)

Contents (continued)

Contents (continued)

Contents (continued)

Figures

Figures (continued)

Tables

Tables (continued)

Appendixes

The appendixes to this report are found in two volumes:

- *Water Quality Vital Signs Monitoring Protocol for the Pacific Island Network: Appendixes*

- *Water Quality Vital Signs Monitoring Protocol for the Pacific Island Network. Appendix N: Water Quality Monitoring Database User Guide.*

Appendix A. Park Background Information for Current Strategic Plans

Appendix B. Revision History Log

Appendix C. Permits and Permission

Appendix D. Sampling Frame

Appendix E. Field Data Form

Appendix F. Water Quality Research Within and Adjacent to Pacific Island Network Park Boundaries

Appendix G. GPRA Goals Addressed by the PACN Water Quality Protocol

Appendix H. State, Territorial, and Commonwealth Water Quality Criteria

Appendix I. State, Regional, and Commonwealth 303(d) Listed Waters

Appendix J. Personnel Names and Contact Information

Appendix K. Roles and Responsibilities

Appendix L. Yearly Project Task List

Appendix M. Database Documentation

Appendix N. Water Quality Database User's Guide

Standard Operating Procedures

The appendixes to this report are found in the volume *Water Quality Vital Signs Monitoring Protocol for the Pacific Island Network: Standard Operating Procedures.*

SOP 1. General Preparations for Field Work

SOP 2. Training Technicians

SOP 3. Safety Protocol

SOP 4. Using Garmin Global Positioning Systems (GPS) Units

SOP 5. Pre-Sampling Equipment Preparation

SOP 6. Selecting Water Quality Sampling Stations

SOP 7. Conducting Water Quality Sampling

SOP 8. Post-Field Work Procedures and Equipment Maintenance

SOP 9. Quality Assurance Project Plan

SOP 10. Workspace setup and Project Records Management

SOP 11. Field Form Handling Procedures

SOP 12. Managing Photographic Images

SOP 13. Data Entry and Verification

SOP 14. Post-season Data Quality Review and Certification

SOP 15. Metadata Development

SOP 16. Sensitive Information Procedures

SOP 17. Product Delivery Specifications

SOP 18. Product Posting and Distribution

SOP 19. Data Analysis and Reporting

SOP 20. Revising the Protocol

Acronym List for Water Quality Vital Sign Protocol Narrative

ALKA: Ala Kahakai National Historic Trail (West Hawaii)

AMME: American Memorial Park (Saipan, CMNI)

ASEPA: American Samoa Environmental Protection Agency

CNMI: Commonwealth of the Northern Mariana Islands

COLA: cost-of-living adjustment

CV: coefficient of variation

CWA: Clean Water Act

DO: dissolved oxygen

DOH: Department of Health

EMAP: Environmental Monitoring and Assessment Program

FGDC: Federal Geographic Data Committee

FOIA: Freedom of Information Act

FTE: full-time equivalent

GIS: geographic information system

GPRA: Government Performance and Results Act

GPS: global positioning system

GRTS: generalized random tessellation stratified

HALE: Haleakala National Park (Maui)

HAVO: Hawaii Volcanoes National Park (East Hawaii)

HPI-CESU: Hawaii-Pacific Islands Cooperative Ecosystems Studies Unit

I&M: Inventory and Monitoring

KAHO: Kaloko-Honokohau National Historical Park (West Hawaii)

KALA: Kalaupapa National Historical Park (Molokai)

NELHA: Natural Energy Lab of Hawaii Authority

NHP: National Historical Park

NO$_3$: Nitrate

NPS: National Parks Service

NPSA: National Park of American Samoa (American Samoa)

NPS-WRD: National Parks Service-Water Resources Division

NRC: Natural Resource Challenge

NRTR: Natural Resource Technical Report

ONRW: outstanding natural resource waters

PACN: Pacific Island Network

PCBs: polychlorinated biphenyls

PICRP: NPS Pacific Island Coral Reef Program

PL: project lead

PUHE: Pu'ukohola Heiau National Historical Site (West Hawaii)

PUHO: Pu'uhonua o Honaunau National Historical Park (West Hawaii)

QA: quality assurance

QC: quality control

SOP: standard operating procedure

SQL: structured query language

TDN: total dissolved nitrogen

TDP: total dissolved phosphate

TN: total nitrogen

TP: total phosphate

USAR: USS Arizona Memorial (Oahu)

USEPA: United States Environmental Protection Agency

USGS: United States Geological Survey

USGS-WRD: United States Geological Survey-Water Resources Division

VIP: Volunteers-in-Parks

WAPA: War in the Pacific National Historical Park (Guam)

WQS: water quality standards

Executive Summary

Water resources in the Pacific Island Network (PACN) support rich and diverse ecosystems and aquatic communities that include corals reefs, anchialine pools communities (endemic to Hawaii), and freshwater stream communities. These water resources span a range of conditions from pristine to highly impaired water bodies. Both point and non-point sources impact the waters of many of our network parks at various locations (DeVerse and DiDonato 2006) to varying degrees. Aquatic resource protection is required by all the governments of the PACN, and water quality is widely used as an indicator of aquatic resource condition by regulators and ecologists. The United States Clean Water Act (CWA) of 1977 requires States and Territories to promulgate legally enforceable water quality standards (WQS) and lists of waters not currently meeting or expected to meet the standards. This protocol should provide the parks with some of the summary information necessary to determine their compliance with the applicable WQS in addition to providing correlative environmental data to ecologists. The water quality vital sign is closely linked with the benthic marine community, marine fish, groundwater, and freshwater animal communities vital signs, and monitoring efforts will be conducted in parallel to maximize data value.

The water quality protocol will be implemented in all PACN parks. This protocol provides the methodology for addressing two monitoring questions: 1) What are the ranges and variances of the network water quality parameters within selected water bodies? 2) What are the temporal and spatial trends of the network core water quality parameters for individual water bodies or water resource types in each park? The first question has the objective to determine the range and spatial variance on an annual basis of temperature, pH, conductivity/salinity, dissolved oxygen (DO), turbidity, total dissolved nitrogen (TDN), total dissolved phosphorous (TDP), Nitrate (NO_3), and chlorophyll in coastal marine waters, streams, wetlands, and a saline lake in the 11 PACN parks. The second question has the objective of determining the temporal (events, diurnal, seasonal, annual, decadal) and spatial trends, for the temperature, pH, conductivity/salinity, and dissolved oxygen in coastal marine waters, streams, and wetlands in the 11 PACN parks.

This protocol employs a split panel design with eight fixed and random sites sampled quarterly along with two extended deployment sondes collecting physical parameters seasonally (wet and dry seasons) in each monitored park water resource. This design provides for the ability to provide both status and trend information. This design also statistically increases the power to detect change over time, resulting from the ability to conduct parameter corrections based on repeat analysis. In addition, the utilization of extended deployment sondes maximizes the ability to use data to conduct trend analyses. This sampling regime represents the maximum sustainable effort given current fiscal realities for the I&M water quality monitoring program only. Increased sampling is possible with more assistance from parks, in addition to partnering with other federal, state, territorial, or local water quality monitoring programs, including interested and reliable non-governmental and private organizations.

Personnel requirements for this vital signs monitoring effort identify a team approach from a variety of organizational levels. Individual park staff provides some in-park coordination for field efforts while the PACN Aquatic Ecologist serves as the project lead and supervises a Biological Technician. The PACN Aquatic Ecologist is the primary park-based liaison ensuring this vital signs monitoring effort continues to address park management needs. The Biological Technician assists the Aquatic Ecologist in coordination efforts and is responsible for pre- and post- season preparations, assisting each park with field work, and conducting the bulk of initial data management, quality assurance, and analysis. The PACN Aquatic Ecologist and other PACN staff help facilitate vital sign monitoring operations, ensure database management, conduct detailed status and trend analyses and reporting, and provide other reporting and operational assistance at a network and national level.

The complete Water Quality Vital signs Monitoring Protocol consists of this narrative and additional volumes containing appendixes and standard operating procedures. Any changes in this narrative will be logged in the revision history log found in Appendix B. This protocol shall not be altered for the sole purpose of becoming compatible with a short-term (20 years or less) state or regional water quality monitoring program.

Acknowledgements

This vital signs monitoring protocol and associated Standard Operating Procedures (SOPs) were prepared with assistance from the Hawaii-Pacific Islands Cooperative Ecosystems Studies Unit (HPI-CESU) and NPS Pacific Island Coral Reef Program (PICRP). It would also not have been possible without the willing support of park-based staff including Stephen Anderson, Elizabeth Gordon, Dwayne Minton, Sarah Creachbaum, Jenny Drake, Tammy Duchesne, Peter Craig, Paul Brown, Epi Suafoa, Lina Fuamatu, Fale Tuilagi, Risé Hart, Sallie Beavers, Lisa Marrick, Rebecca Most, Malia Laber, and Chuck Sayon.

1 - Background and Objectives

The Natural Resource Challenge (NRC), initiated in 1999 under the auspices of the Omnibus Act (1998), an action plan for preserving natural resources throughout the National Park Service (NPS). To meet the goals of the NRC, the NPS established 32 Inventory and Monitoring (I&M) networks, including 270 National Park units, to better economize their funding. Each network is comprised of NPS units that share geographical and natural resource characteristics, allowing these parks to share financial resources and expertise (NPS 2006a). The Inventory and Monitoring Program's first objective was to complete basic inventories of natural resources in all parks. This information formed the baseline information for long-term monitoring efforts. Because program funding is limited and not everything within park ecosystems can be monitored, monitoring programs were built around measuring critical parameters (vital signs) within each network in order to gauge ecosystem health. The information gained by monitoring will be used for natural resource management decision-making.

As defined by the NPS, vital signs are a subset of physical, chemical, and biological elements and processes of park ecosystems that are selected to represent the overall health or condition of park resources, known or hypothesized effects of stressors, or elements that have important human values. This subset of monitored resources and processes is part of the total suite of natural resources that park managers are directed to preserve "unimpaired for future generations" (National Park Service Organic Act of 1916), including water, air, geological resources, plants and animals, and the various ecological, biological, and physical processes that act on those resources." Major challenges addressed in the NRC pertinent to aquatic environments include native and endangered species, non-native species, environmental stewardship, and water quality. The PACN Vital Signs Monitoring Plan and this protocol address these issues.

Water quality monitoring is widely used as an indicator of aquatic resource condition by regulators and ecologists and will contribute to Pacific Island Network (PACN) parks' ability to realize goals pertaining to the Government Performance and Results Act (GPRA). Not all PACN parks have GPRA goals specifically relating to water quality, yet, many parks value access to water quality information and better managed aquatic habitats (specific GPRA goals for each PACN park are listed in Appendix G of this protocol, along with an explanation of how water quality monitoring will assist parks in attaining these goals). Examples of how water quality monitoring relates to PACN parks' GPRA goals and strategic plans include: wetland habitat restoration and management, recreational opportunities in and around aquatic resources, protected habitat for federally listed endangered or threatened aquatic species, compliance with WQS and associated habitat protection, and preservation/restoration of cultural resources such as Hawaiian fishponds. In addition to GPRA goals, legislation requiring specific water quality standards has been created by all of the government entities encompassing the PACN.

The most significant legislation applicable to water quality is the United States Clean Water Act (CWA) of 1977. The CWA requires States and Territories to identify and publish water quality standards (WQS) as well as identify waters that do not currently meet or are not expected to meet the adopted standards. The resulting Federal, State, Territorial, and Commonwealth regulations on water quality standards provide a framework for designating and protecting water bodies for specific uses (Guam Environmental Protection Agency 2001, Commonwealth of the Northern

Mariana Islands Department of Environmental Quality 2004, American Samoa Environmental Protection Agency 1999, State of Hawaii Department of Health 2004). These WQS include numeric criteria for fresh and marine water bodies. The legislation for each region covers other water resources mandating protection from pollution and degradation although numeric criteria are not available. Guam and CNMI include protection of groundwater resources in their regulations and wetlands are specifically addressed in the CNMI WQS. In the absence of national water quality criteria for marine waters, we will follow those of the State of Hawaii Department of Health (DOH).

1.1 Location
The PACN is comprised of 11 National Park units (Appendix A, Appendix D) spread across the tropical Pacific Ocean between 25°N and 20°S latitude (Figure 1). These units are all coastally located on relatively small islands and governed by four different entities; the Territory of Guam, the Commonwealth of the Northern Mariana Islands (CNMI), the Territory of American Samoa, and the State of Hawaii. These Pacific island entities are made up of relatively small and physically disconnected island communities. The individual islands of the PACN all share a tropical climate, remote location, and significant influence from indigenous cultures, but vary widely within these attributes. Variations in natural (precipitation, topography) and human (demographics, industry) factors combine differently in each locale; however, the quality of surface waters, marine waters, and groundwater is critical to the functioning of both aquatic and terrestrial systems across the network.

1.2 Threats and Concerns
Water resources in all national park units span a range of conditions from pristine to highly impaired water bodies. Both point and non-point sources impact the waters at various locations (DeVerse and DiDonato 2006). Network-wide concerns for these resources include atmospheric deposition, changes in hydrology and climate, chemical and microbial contamination, organic and inorganic enrichment, invasive species, erosion, and sedimentation. Almost all PACN parks are susceptible to the effects of feral animals that degrade native vegetation and increase erosion. Natural disturbance events contribute to the transfer of sediment and chemicals from land into nearby streams, groundwater, and marine resources. Solar radiation and ambient temperature affect water quantity and quality, and as a result, the well-being of organisms living in impacted areas (Sutherland et al. 2004).

Unfortunately, many of the drivers which impact the water quality of parks within the PACN take place outside of park jurisdictional boundaries. Most, if not all, PACN parks are concerned about development of adjacent lands and watersheds. Expansion of urban land use often affects the hydrology of nearby ecosystems by diversion of streams and withdrawal of groundwater (USGS-WRD 2003). Human population growth contributes to loss of habitat buffers and subsequent degradation of water quality. Construction and recreation activities contribute to erosion, pollution, and the introduction of alien species. Chemicals from land-based sources enter groundwater via surface water connections possibly contaminating drinking water supplies and eventually coastal resources (De Carlo et al. 2000).

Adjacent land uses have impacts on the marine environment as well (Houk 2001, Sutherland et al. 2004), and all PACN parks have nearshore reef communities that may be influenced by situations inside or outside of park boundaries. Moreover, PACN parks do not have jurisdiction over the submerged lands containing reef resources that they are mandated to protect (that responsibility belongs to the state or territory).

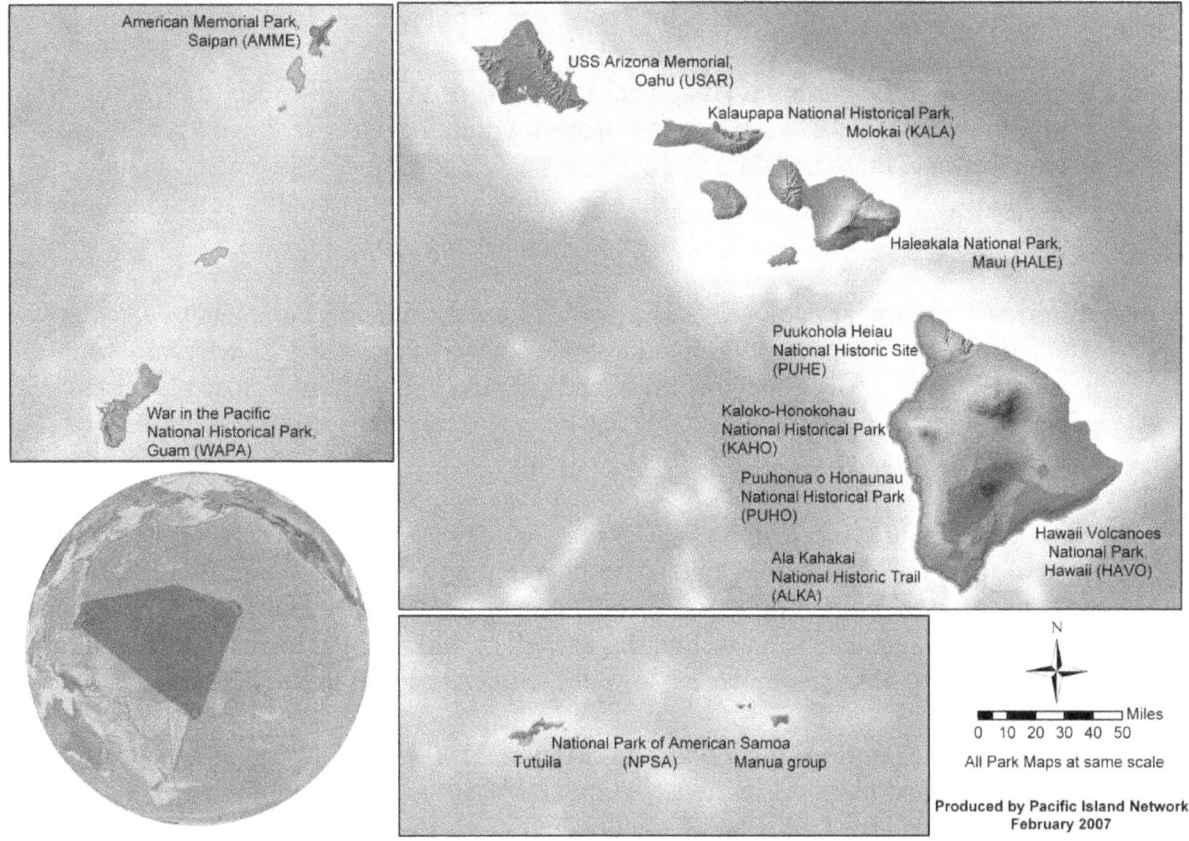

Figure 1. Map showing the geographical region of the 11 Pacific Island Network park units. The PACN covers a large geographical area in the Tropical Pacific Ocean and is governed by four different entities; the Territory of Guam, the Commonwealth of the Northern Mariana Islands (CNMI), the Territory of American Samoa, and the State of Hawaii.

Harbor operations, such as boat maintenance and fueling facilities contribute to chemical pollution in these areas by increasing the presence of paints, solvents, diesel, oils, and heavy metals. The operation of cruise ships, commercial fishing, and diving charters raises the likelihood of illegal dumping of chemicals, sewage, and debris. Three of the west Hawaii parks, PUHE, KAHO, and ALKA, are adjacent to state harbors that are in the planning stages for expansion which may intensify threats to the marine community such as fishing pressure, introduction of alien algae and invertebrates, boat groundings, and other physical damage to reef resources from increased recreational activities. Runoff from agricultural and urban development and sedimentation due to natural and anthropogenic causes increases eutrophication, bacterial and chemical contamination, and turbidity (Fabricius 2005).

Rising sea levels and storm surge may accelerate shoreline erosion resulting in increased sedimentation of reefs and changes in coastal habitat. Natural impacts include island subsidence and rising sea level, which will ultimately contribute to erosion of the shoreline at many PACN parks. Coral bleaching, mortality, and disease also are occurring due to warming sea surface temperatures, sedimentation, and water pollution (Hoegh-Guldberg 1999, Craig and Basch 2001, Houk 2001, Sutherland et al. 2004). Through surveys of NPS staff, partners, and other media, each park has identified the stressors which most threaten their water resources. Listed below are brief summaries of water resources and issues within each of the PACN parks.

- **War in the Pacific National Historical Park (WAPA)** contains over 1,000 acres of marine area, a wetland, and numerous streams within the park. Sedimentation, intense fishing, sewage, litter, and the presence of relic WWII military equipment, including large numbers of unexploded ordinance are some of the water quality concerns for this park.

- **American Memorial Park (AMME)** has no submerged lands, but contains an extensive wetland with native mangroves. In addition to threats associated with terrestrial runoff, areas offshore of AMME may be impacted by contaminants from a closed landfill adjacent to the park. The wetland area has been severely impacted by historical land uses. Sea level rise is also a concern to this low-lying park.

- **National Park of American Samoa (NPSA)** contains extensive coral reefs and pristine streams that may be impacted by rapid population growth in the region. Water quality at NPSA is affected by non-point source pollution, groundwater withdrawal, bacteria, and nutrients from human and animal wastes as well as other contaminants. Global climate change and the subsequent increase in water temperature are also of concern.

- **USS Arizona Memorial Park National Memorial (USAR)** consists of a visitor center, a parking lot, and joint jurisdiction with the US Navy over two submerged vessels: the USS Arizona and the USS Utah. This jurisdiction does not extend to the surrounding marine area of Pearl Harbor, which is a heavily altered embayment due to extensive and long-standing Naval operations and increasing urban development. There are several hundred thousand gallons of Bunker C fuel oil encased in the hull of the USS Arizona with catastrophic potential if released.

- **Kalaupapa National Historical Park (KALA)** legislative boundary extends a quarter mile offshore, and encompasses relatively pristine marine resources and two offshore islands. Threatened and endangered sea turtles forage within the park, and endangered monk seals use the beaches. Coral reefs are threatened by sedimentation and agricultural runoff. The primary concerns for freshwater resources of this park are invasive species, erosion, and diversion of streams to supply upland development. This park boasts a crater lake with unique water quality characteristics.

- **Haleakala National Park (HALE)** boundary ends at the high tide line but has extensive and somewhat isolated intertidal regions, coastal springs, lakes, bogs, and pristine isolated streams. Stream diversion, invasive species, erosion, and encroaching development are the main impacts to water quality in this park.

- **Ala Kahakai National Historic Trail (ALKA)** is a 175 mile trail corridor traversing the west Hawaii coast from the northern Upolu Point south to Ka Lae, and continuing up the eastern side of Hawaii Island through Hawaii Volcanoes National Park. The water quality issues for ALKA vary with the changing land uses on Hawaii Island. Although this trail system does not technically include the nearshore marine areas, harbor operations, runoff, and groundwater quality are concerns for the coastal waters in developed areas.

- **Puukohola Heiau National Historic Site (PUHE)** administrative boundary stops at the high tide line, although the enabling legislation intended that it extend into the marine area of Pelekane Bay. The park has an ephemeral brackish water pond located in an otherwise dry gulch that is impacted by flood events during periods of high rainfall upslope. Upland development and ranching contribute to erosion, runoff and associated sedimentation of Pelekane Bay. Consequently, this bay is now listed as an impaired water body by the Hawaii Department of Health. Kawaihae Harbor is adjacent to the park and is slated for expansion which may increase nearshore sedimentation and restrict water flow.

- **Kaloko-Honokohau National Historical Park (KAHO)** contains approximately 10% of the anchialine pools on Hawaii Island. In addition, there are three fish ponds, and a large embayment down-slope of a growing industrial area. Adjacent land use may contribute to contamination and nutrient loading of the groundwater that feeds the wetlands, anchialine pools, and subsequently the marine waters. These aquatic resources are affected ecologically when introduced species alter the environment. A small boat harbor is located south of the park and is a source of petroleum, heavy metals, and other contaminants. The threat of sedimentation onto the coral reef is increased by pond restoration activities, erosion of the sandy shoreline, and dredging and/or future expansion of the harbor. Upslope development and groundwater uptake are also threats to this coastal park. Unfortunately, KAHO administers the marine area but does not have "law enforcement jurisdiction" over the marine resources.

- **Puuhonua o Honaunau National Historical Park (PUHO)** boundary ends at the high tide line. Urban development up-slope from the park and the high level of tourism can have an impact on the water quality (sediment, nutrients, and contaminants) of springs, fishponds, anchialine pools, and the nearshore marine environment. Sedimentation and the introduction of alien fish in the fishponds and anchialine pools have contributed to their decline. Island subsidence and the rising sea level, due to global climate change, may eventually lead to flooding in this low coastal park.

- **Hawaii Volcanoes National Park (HAVO)** boundary ends at the high tide line, limiting its aquatic resources to coastal intertidal areas, anchialine pools, and bogs in the upland rainforest. No known streams or lakes exist in this park, which is primarily made up of relatively young volcanic flows. Although the coastal area is large, the threat of runoff from paved areas is limited by the volcanic activity, the main agent of change in this park.

1.3 Potential PACN Management Implications

When a specified water quality parameter exceeds federal, state, local, territorial, or commonwealth water criteria, a trigger point for management action has been reached (Appendix

H). This means that water resources are no longer in compliance with relevant water quality standards. It is up to the managers to decide whether they want to pursue an action, delay, or ignore. This is a point we want to avoid, and monitoring water quality for declining trends informs managers, enhancing their ability to avert this situation prior to having to answer questions as to why their resource is impaired; a fear of all NPS managers/superintendents. Any significant trend in water quality parameter decline should be a trigger for informing management of the declining situation. Nevertheless, because issues may be of a larger scale than park management can deal with, options for management are often limited. Nevertheless, knowing system linkages is imperative to making informed management decisions to avoid, avert, or improve declining resource status.

A monitoring program for marine, freshwater, and brackish water resources will provide a system-wide understanding of the current status of water resources allowing prioritization and improved management of threatened resources. Once problem areas are identified, park management can begin the process of prioritization necessary to address park resource needs. Scientific information can be used to guide rational and responsible management actions and policies relating to the environment and should be readily available for resource managers to identify stressors and potential causes of change.

Understanding the system linkages affecting water quality, and subsequent trend information gathered through monitoring, will aid NPS park managers in their ability to target potential problem areas that can be addressed using their managerial influences (Figure 2), within and external to park jurisdictional boundaries. Results from monitoring will inform management decisions at differing scales; global, regional, or park. Stressors originating within park boundaries can be addressed through direct management action; stressors originating outside park boundaries may need to be addressed through indirect means, such as influencing other jurisdictional agencies and decision makers through partnerships or commenting on proposed development activities. Regardless of the chosen management action, the NPS will have scientifically credible monitoring results available to inform the public, upper management, legislators, and international communities about their concerns and recommendations.

1.4 Conceptual Models

Conceptual models are used to better understand the context of a given vital sign. The I&M Program uses two general types of conceptual models: stressor models and control models (Gross 2003). Stressor models help to identify the relationships between stressors (drivers), ecosystem components, and effects. However, these models do not typically incorporate the actual mechanisms of the interactions; instead, they are generally descriptive and retrospective. In contrast, control models represent key processes, interactions, and feedbacks (Gross 2003). In the context of PACN protocols, control models are likely to serve as a stronger foundation for understanding the mechanistic functioning of the ecosystem.

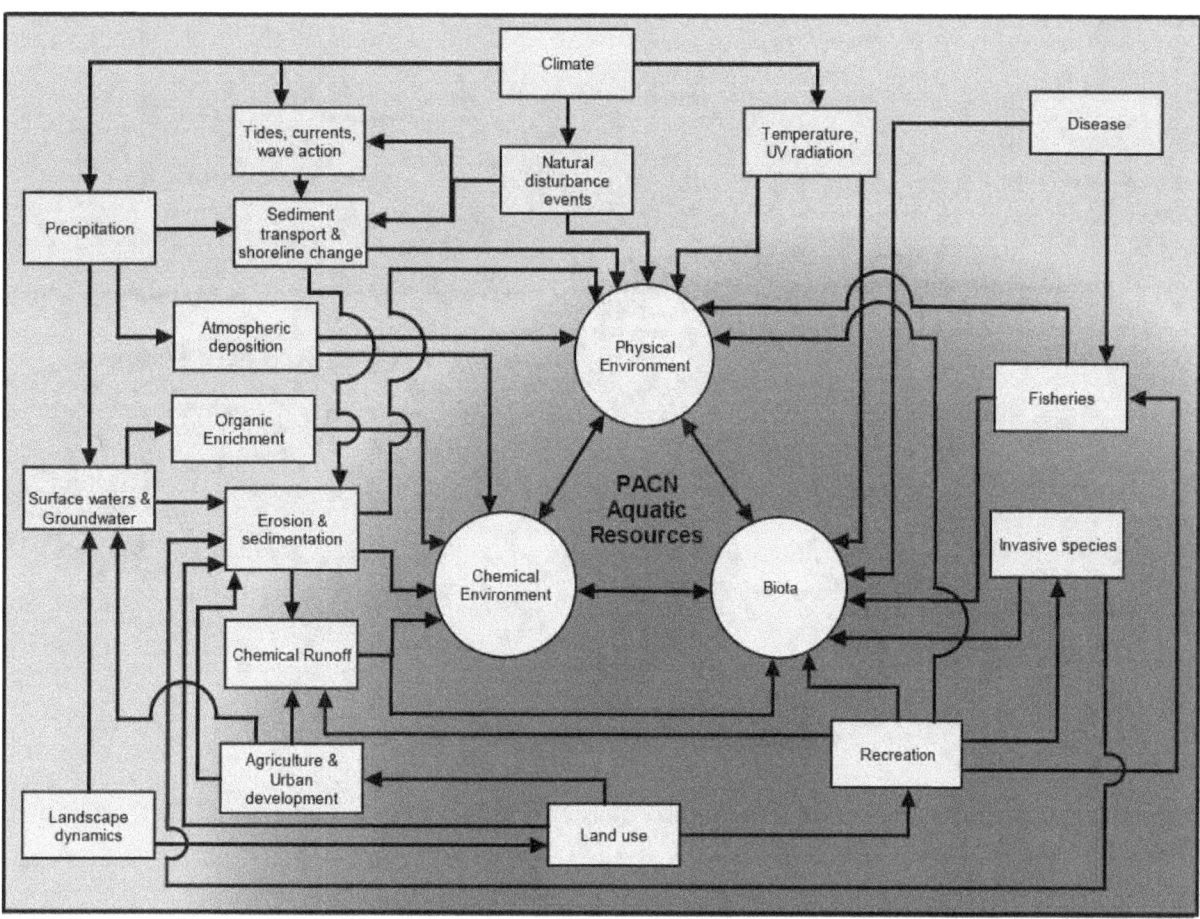

Figure 2. Managerial influences relative to select aquatic resource stressors and their interactions. The managerial influence is indicated in green. Boxes within the green may be directly influenced by park management decisions. Boxes in the grey area must be influenced by other means. Colored boxes indicate stressors, orange circles indicate the aquatic resource component, and arrows indicate linkages. Please note these are not all stressors or linkages.

1.4.1 Water Quality

From the tops of the mountains to the ocean floor, water plays a significant role in defining the physical, chemical, and biological components of an ecosystem. On Pacific islands, freshwater enters the ecosystem initially through rain, snow, or fog (primarily rain). The water then either infiltrates the ground or runs off the land and into streams or the ocean. Infiltrated water recharges aquifers and travels as groundwater through the rocks, eventually resurfacing in streams or discharging into the ocean, where oceanic currents then move the water and associated physical and chemical components. Water reenters the atmosphere through evapotranspiration and the process repeats. The potential for extraneous organic and inorganic inputs exist at each point along the progression of water from rain to sea, altering the water quality and characteristics with each input (Figure 3).

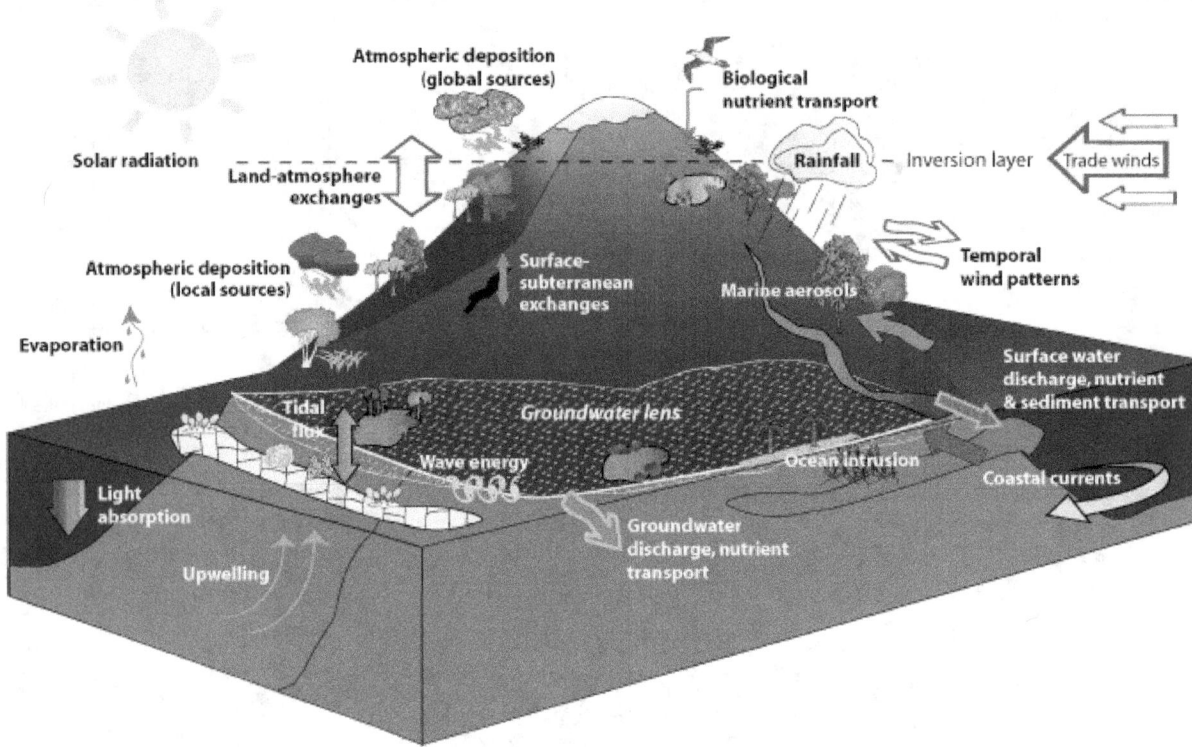

Figure 3. Natural pathways and sources of water quality contamination on a generalized Pacific island (HaySmith et al. 2006).

The water quality and characteristics associated with each watershed are altered significantly by the chemical, biological, and land use practices found within. Anthropogenic and natural changes through point and non-point source inputs to the watershed, alter water quality by changing physical, chemical, and/or biological components and quantities entering the water supply. Point source inputs are those that can be traced to a specific area such as a sewage pipe or industrial dump site, while non-point source inputs like agricultural run-off or animal droppings provide inputs over large areas (Figure 4).

Urban and agricultural development of adjacent lands and watersheds affect almost all PACN parks. Human population growth contributes to loss of habitat buffers and subsequent degradation of water quality. Alteration of watersheds and associated changes in vegetative cover often decrease the ability of the land to absorb rainfall resulting in increased runoff. Generally, runoff from developed watersheds carries higher sediment loads than from undeveloped areas, and this effect is more pronounced in areas where the topography is characterized by steep slopes.

Water from urban and agricultural development absorbed into the groundwater contains increased chemical and microbial contaminants as compared to native systems, eventually discharging into coastal resources such as anchialine pools, nearshore coral reefs, and wetlands. Figure 5 illustrates groundwater and surface water movement on volcanic islands, as well as sources and pathways of pollutant movement.

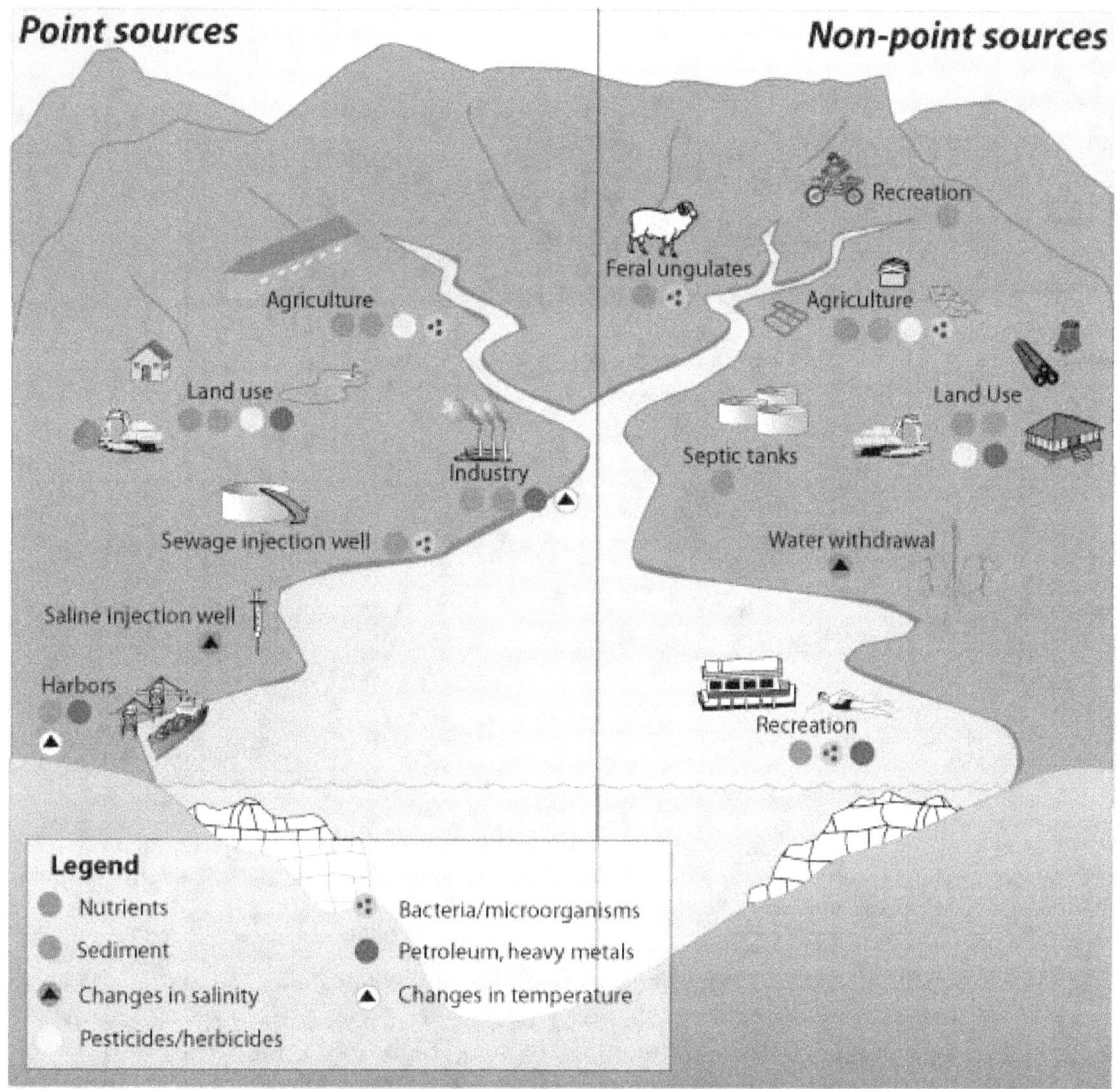

Figure 4. Examples of point and non-point source pollution found within the Pacific islands along with the associated types of pollution each source contributes to overall water quality (Deverse and Didonato 2006).

From incidental chemical inputs to habitat modification, all alterations to water quality have some effect on the ecosystem (Figure 6), and the greatest concerns are the intensity and length of time that a stressor is present in the system. High intensity stressors can cause significant, immediately recognizable changes (i.e. an oil spill) while low intensity stressors can take years to identify (i.e. climate change). The longer a stressor is present (i.e. slow removal of oil from a spill), the greater the impact to the organisms that inhabit the ecosystem, and the longer their recovery time. In addition, the greater the effect a stressor has on the ecosystem as a whole, the longer the recovery time (Figure 7). For instance, increased acidification may destabilize geologic formations, increase erosion, and release trace metals and other contaminants into the watershed. Unfortunately, water quality stressors tend to be chronic and of low intensity making them difficult to detect; and the consequent recovery of a system also slow.

9

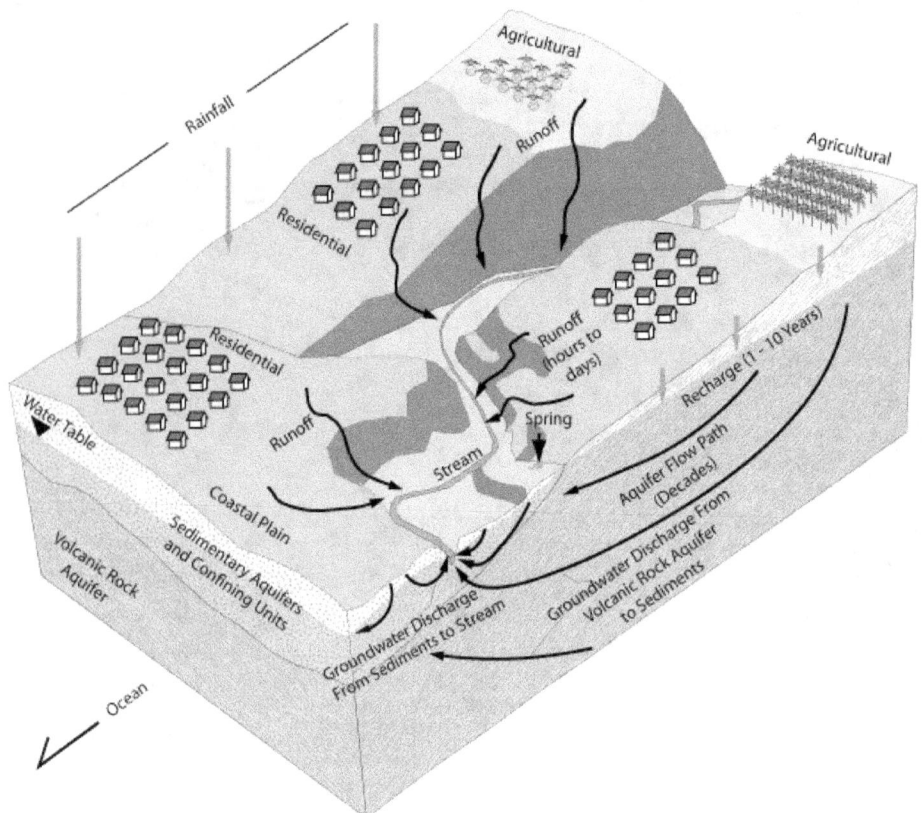

Figure 5. Schematic of groundwater and surface water movement on volcanic islands, illustrating pollution pathways (modified from Anthony et al. 2004). In this diagram, the mountainside slopes from the top right to the ocean at bottom left.

The delays in recovery time are directly associated with the way water quality affects ecosystems as a whole. Water quality can cause and be altered by landscape level changes, yet affects the biotic integrity of a system on cellular and organismal levels (Figure 8). If the stressors are adequately managed, these effects can be reduced, but if ignored, or unknown, they begin to spread their effect up the hierarchical levels of an ecosystem (Figure 8), eventually causing landscape level changes. For restoration and management efforts to be effective, it must be understood that the length of time required to effectively restore an ecosystem is proportional to the length of time that the stressor causing the ecosystem change has been occurring. Because the duration of ecosystem recovery time is so long, but the effects of water quality change are often slow to be realized, water quality monitoring in the PACN is crucial to effectively managing the parks' ecosystems. By identifying the stressors and their degree of change, it may be possible for mangers to attempt mitigation prior to larger scale ecosystem changes.

While it is not feasible to monitor the myriad of parameters that affect water quality, this monitoring can be accomplished by focusing on some of the core parameters that are known to affect different ecosystems. Since many water bodies may be unique to their park and have water quality issues due to specific stresses, research and monitoring requirements will need to be addressed individually. The PACN vital sign "Water Quality" addresses these concerns, and ultimately, water quality monitoring should be capable of giving park management officials time to consider options based on the known degree of change occurring within their park.

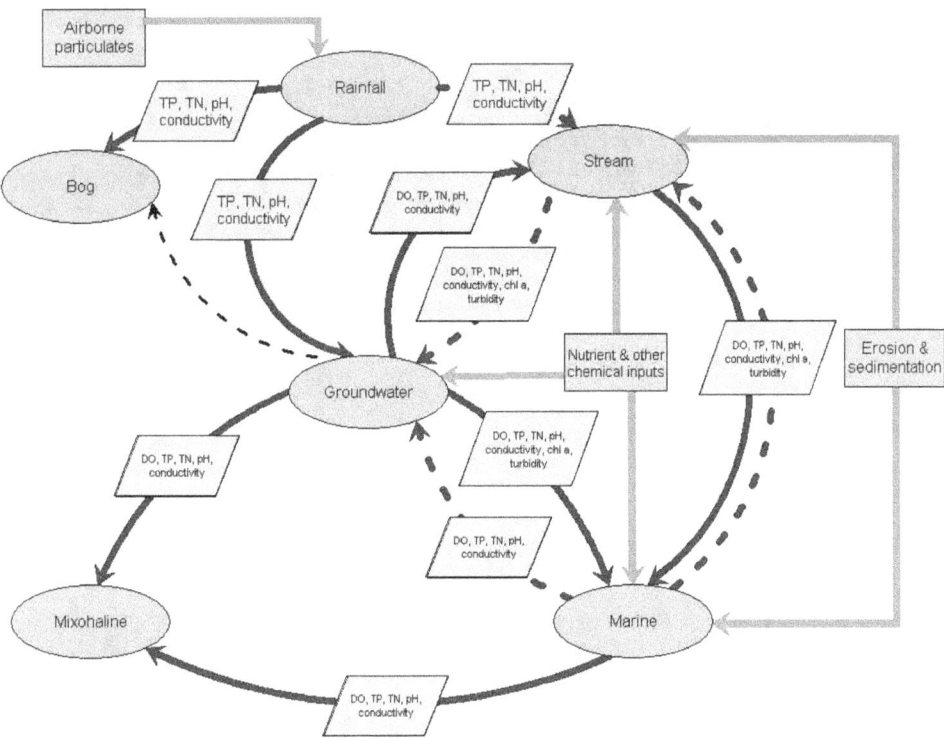

Figure 6. Some water quality parameters (trapezoids) and their linkages to the ecosystem (ovals). Less significant conduits are drawn with dotted arrows. Stressors (rectangles) to the ecosystem are shown as well.

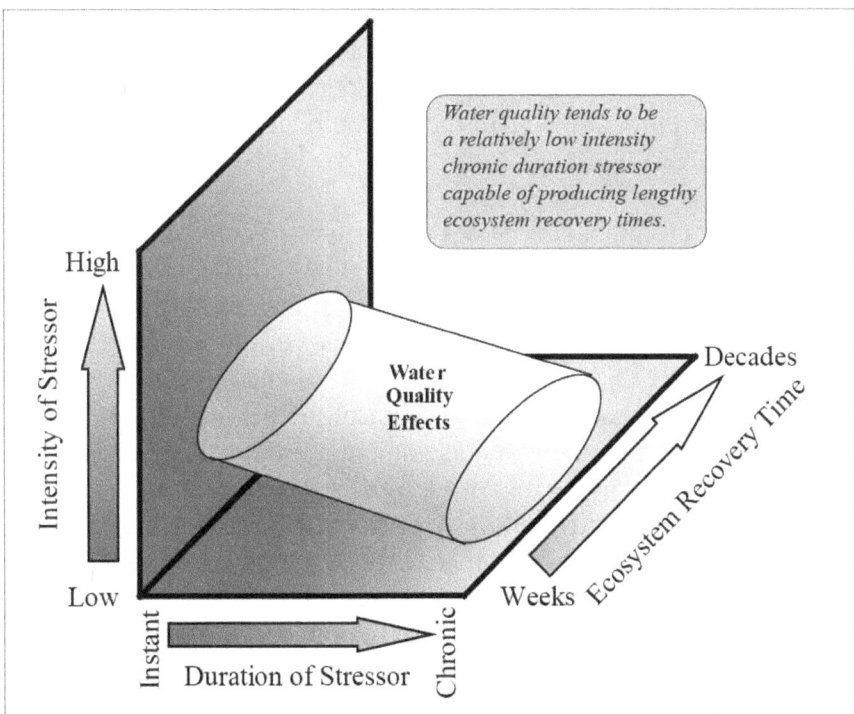

Figure 7. Duration, intensity, and ecosystem recovery time for water quality changes.

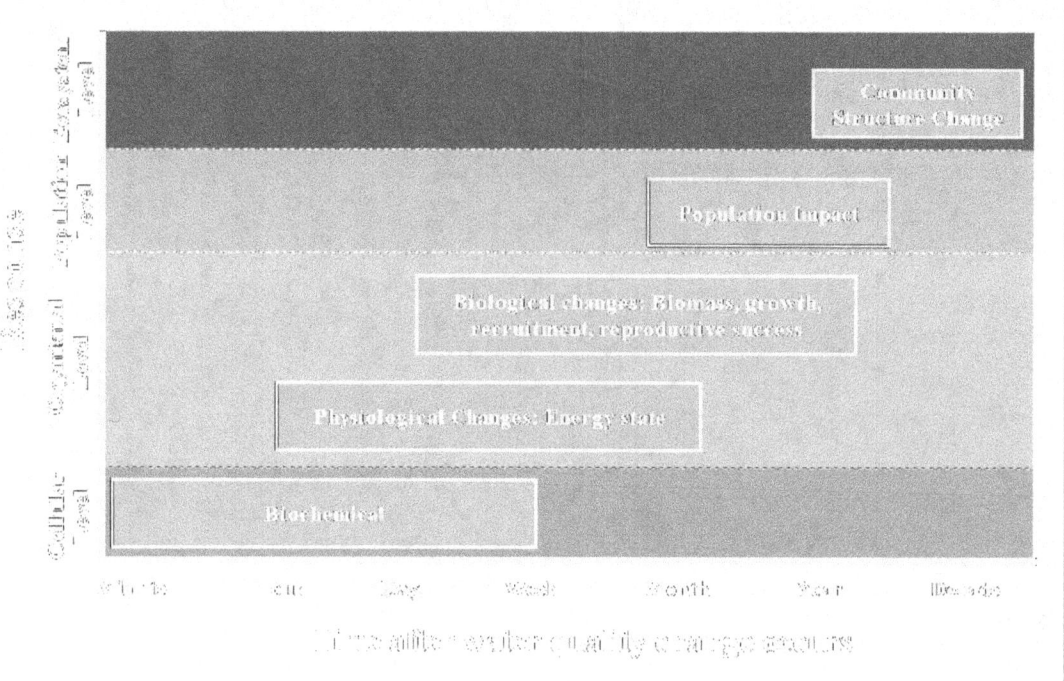

Figure 8. Duration of water quality changes and their effects at differing hierarchical ecosystem levels.

1.4.2 Drivers and Stressors

Drivers and stressors are factors that directly influence the environment and may have human or natural origins (Figure 9). Stressors are changes in natural conditions that result from the operation of a driver. At local spatial scales, drivers can occur independently of one another, but often operate simultaneously, magnifying the effect of associated stressors on the ecosystem. This is indicated in the conceptual model by enclosure of the stressors into one box relating to ecosystem responses. In the interest of including all water types, this model represents a very broad explanation of aquatic systems.

Climate Change: Change in climate refers to global processes that affect ambient conditions in such a way that prospective conditions differ from recorded historical ones. Parks in the PACN are coastal parks susceptible to rising sea level, such as with global warming and the thermal expansion of seawater (Wetherald 1991). In the PACN, nearshore reefs, coastal wetlands, anchialine pools, and historical fishponds are the water bodies most threatened by changes in sea level. Changes in sea level affect shoreline dynamics and hydrological factors leading to inundation and erosion of coastlines (Leatherman 1991) and sedimentation of nearshore areas. The impact to areas susceptible to seawater intrusion into drinking water sources is also important because of salt contamination and the difficulties involved with removing salt from drinking water. Terrestrial ecosystems may experience similar changes in composition and structure resulting from saltwater intrusion, storm damage, flooding, and changes in precipitation due to climatic influences (Leatherman 1991). Nearshore habitats may undergo regime shifts when temperatures are no longer tolerable for corals, leading to changes in benthic habitat, species composition, and offshore topography (Smith et al. 2001).

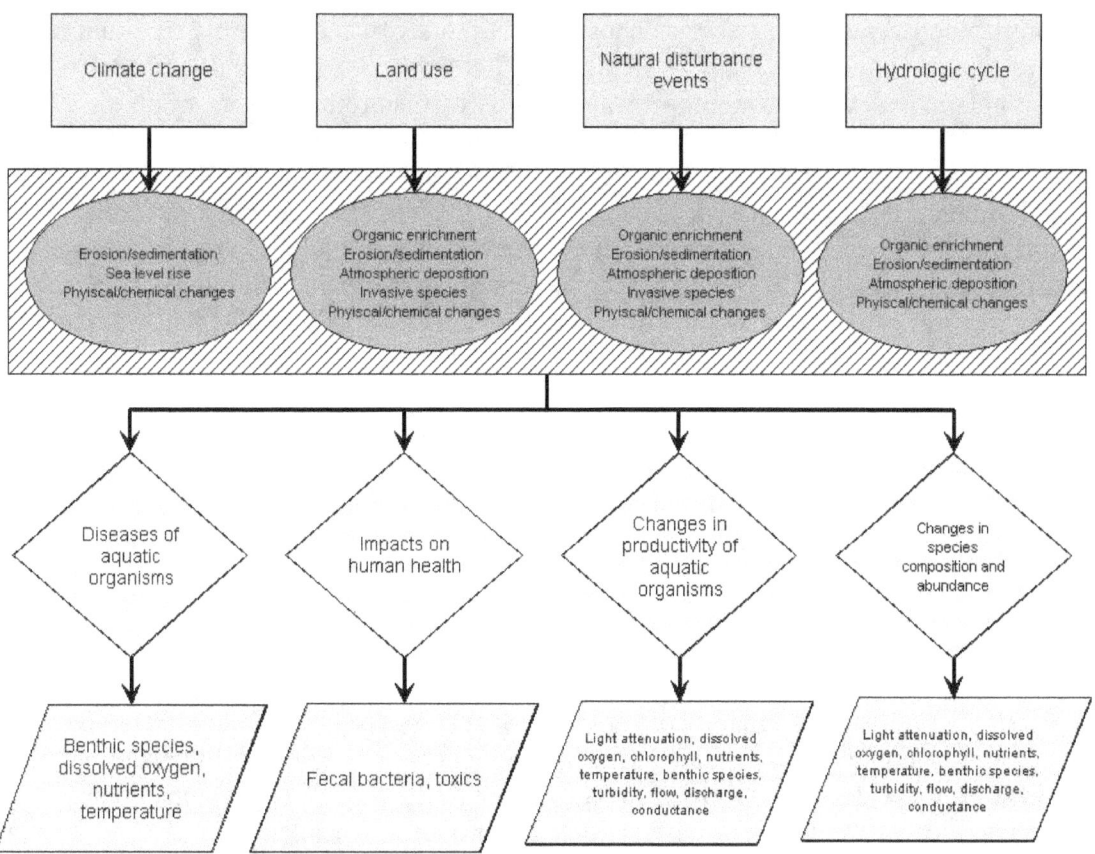

Figure 9. Whole ecosystem linkages in the PACN water quality model and their measures. Drivers (blue boxes), stressors (red ovals), ecosystem responses (yellow diamonds), and measures (green parallelograms).

Land Use: Human activity negatively influences water quality (Valiela et al. 1990, Cosser 1997, Hoegh-Guldberg 1999, Houk 2001, USGS-WRD 2003). Organic enrichment and other chemical changes in water quality may occur due to the presence of farms, human waste, waste water systems, solid waste, and landscaped areas. Land use, such as agriculture, construction of roads, piers, and barriers in coastal areas, and stream channelization, contributes to erosion and subsequent sedimentation, with concurrent physical and chemical changes in aquatic environments (De Carlo et al. 2000). Power plants, quarries, vehicles, and construction activities are sources of particulates that cause contamination of water resources through atmospheric deposition, discharges, and storm events. Human population growth and resulting urban development destroys native habitat, often simultaneously introducing new species into disturbed areas where they out-compete the native biota. Large scale removal of vegetation can influence precipitation patterns (Salati and Nobre 1991, Betts 2004) increasing the likelihood that drought, fire, and erosion will contribute to degradation of streams, wetlands, anchialine pools, fishponds, and reefs. Recreational and commercial activities involving fishing, swimming, and boating alter marine and stream resources by influencing species composition and introducing chemical and physical pollutants. Carbon dioxide emissions by industrialized populations and destruction of tropical forests are contributing to global climate change (Ehrlich 1991) which will alter the hydrology of the earth (Wetherald 1991, Hayes 1991, Valiela 1995).

13

Natural Disturbance Events: Atmospheric deposition, earthquakes, and tsunamis are examples of natural events that can have unpredictable effects on water resources. Natural disturbance events such as flooding and high winds can impact water quality by disturbing human structures designed to contain pollutants. Sewers, storm drains, and wastewater treatment plants may overflow into streams causing physical and chemical changes that eventually affect groundwater and/or nearshore receiving waters (De Carlo et al. 2000). Erosion and sedimentation are accelerated during hurricanes and typhoons either directly or through loss of vegetation. Subsequently, ecosystems may be more likely to be repopulated with invasive species. In addition, flowing lava can alter the quality of seawater when the molten rock enters the ocean (Sedwick et al. 1990).

Hydrologic Cycle: Understanding water flow and its rate of movement is an important aspect of water quality monitoring. Water resources may impact one another through direct connections such as a stream entering the ocean, or indirectly as when evaporation falls on terrestrial water bodies as rain or other forms of precipitation (Garrison et al. 1999). Moving water carries its physical and chemical constituents to the receiving body (De Carlo et al. 2000). Furthermore, both the character and the impacts of these constituents are affected by water quantity and flow rate (Li 1988, Lapointe et al. 1990). When a system is operating within natural ranges of water movement, potential stressors are balanced over time by ecosystem processes. Changes in the hydrologic cycle may offset the capacity of a system to recharge itself, resulting in degraded water quality. For example, groundwater reservoirs are recharged by rainfall in undisturbed systems. When groundwater is withdrawn, changes in relative quantity are accompanied by physical and chemical changes that can affect other water bodies dependant on this groundwater supply such as wetlands and anchialine pools.

1.4.3 Ecosystem Responses and Measures of Change
In order to evaluate water resource issues, an understanding of the effects of stressors on the ecosystem is important. Aquatic ecosystem responses were divided into generalized categories represented by diamonds in the model (Figure 9) and described below. Several possible measures of ecological change due to water quality are indicated for each category of ecosystem response. Once the issues of ecosystem changes are described and prioritized, metrics can be applied to test the theorized relationships.

Disease of Aquatic Organisms: Variations in ambient water quality can result in physical stress, poor health, disease, and increased mortality of aquatic organisms (Valiela et al. 1990, Cosser 1997). Bioaccumulation of and exposure to toxins and heavy metals can have adverse effects such as diseases, tumors, and mortality in many types of aquatic life (Long et al. 1995, Brown 2003). Examples of diseases in aquatic organisms include avian botulism, fibropapillomatosis tumors on turtles, and coral diseases. Changes in water quality variables such as elevated water temperature and negative redox potential, in combination with pH ranging from 7.5 to 9.0, have been shown to increase the risk of avian botulism in wetlands (Rocke & Samuel 1999). Poor health may also result from changes in foraging habitat or a decline in the prey base. Monk seals, whales, and dolphins are also susceptible to poor water quality but they are not ideal indicators of local conditions due to their wide-ranging behavior. Stress associated with degraded conditions can impact growth, survival, and reproduction rates among benthic organisms. Subsequent changes in the composition and abundance of benthic communities can be quantified and monitored. Considering their sedentary nature and influential position in the trophic web,

14

benthic invertebrates and algal communities are a logical choice as indicators of ambient water quality conditions (Jameson et al. in press).

Corals are more susceptible to disease when stressed by poor water quality (Houk 2001, Sutherland et al. 2004, Jameson et al. In press). Coral and macroalgae may be smothered by influxes of sediment (Brown 1997, Wolanski et al. 2003) or corals can be bleached by elevated temperatures in the ambient seawater (Brown 1997, Hoegh-Guldberg 1999). Macroalgae may experience increased productivity with elevated water temperatures resulting in the temporary dominance of a particular species (Glenn et al. 1990). Diseases in coral reefs are rapidly becoming a concern in the Pacific as more outbreaks are discovered in areas thought to be pristine, but little is known about the cause (Richardson 1998). White syndrome (a general term for unexplained loss of tissue from the skeleton), black band disease, and coral tumors are examples of coral diseases currently found in the Pacific. White syndrome on Acroporids is one disease that has been found on reefs across the Pacific, occurring in the Northwestern Hawaiian Islands, American Samoa, and on several other South Pacific reefs (Richardson 1998, G. Aeby, personal communication).

Impact on Human Health: When aquatic ecosystems become contaminated, communities reliant on potable water, subsistence fishing or farming, and tourism are impacted. Toxins and microbial contamination, such as ciguatera and "red tide" algal blooms, are already affecting fishing areas and recreational opportunities throughout the Pacific (Cosser 1997). For populations dependent on surface or groundwater supplies for drinking water and irrigation, maintaining the quality of these resources is imperative to sustaining their quality of life.

Although many stressors impact human health, the measurable effects are well-defined with microbial indicators and chemical contaminants such as mercury or PCBs. The majority of long-term aquatic monitoring programs in place are directed at human health parameters. Experts on tropical marine microbiology are currently developing alternatives to microbial water quality criteria for this region due to low confidence in the current United States Environmental Protection Agency (USEPA) sewage pollution indicators, *Escherichia coli* and *Enteroccoci*, for predicting illness rates in coastal recreation areas (Fujioka et al. 1998, Betancourt and Fujioka 2005, Betancourt and Fujioka 2009).

Change in Productivity of Aquatic Organisms: Changes in productivity affect ecosystem processes such as nutrient cycling and the rate of succession, possibly compounding the effect of the stressors themselves. There are many measures and even more methods for describing productivity. Benthic species abundance and composition is often used to characterize an ecosystem in terms of general water quality parameters (Jameson et al. in press). Certain benthic and plankton species need specific conditions of water clarity, nutrient availability (Hodgkiss and Ho 1997), temperature, pH, primary productivity, dissolved oxygen, and salinity. Some changes in these parameters may not directly affect productivity, but are likely a factor, or driver, in the impact of other, related variables in ecosystem processes. For example, knowing the rate of water flow through a system is crucial to tracking the dynamics of nutrient cycling, temperature, salinity, and the accompanying changes in indicators of primary productivity: chlorophyll a, pH, dissolved oxygen, and clarity.

Changes in Species Composition and Abundance: As with primary producers, the composition of other trophic level species and their abundance is a factor of reproduction, growth, and survival that is influenced by environmental stressors (Valiela et al. 1990, Beyers et al. 1999). Changes in ambient water quality can affect community structure in coral reefs (Matson 1986, Brown 1997). In areas where aquatic herbivores are depleted and nutrients are added, algal growth can increase to the point of smothering coral causing mortality and regime shift (Hughes 1994). The close relationship of change in productivity to change in species composition and abundance is reflected by the same array of parameters to describe them. As with change in productivity, some measures are direct indicators of change and some help assess the expected impact of other stressors. For example, benthic surveys are direct indicators of species composition and abundance, but flow or discharge rates control the influx of nutrients and indirectly affect the community being surveyed (Valiela et al. 1990).

1.5 Other Monitoring Efforts Past and Present

To make monitoring both cost-effective and ecologically relevant, co-location of monitoring efforts is desirable. Several related vital signs are well set to provide valuable biological information to aid in the ecological interpretation of this physical and chemical oriented vital sign, particularly in relation to species composition and abundance shifts and coral mortality. In this protocol, co-location efforts include monitoring water quality at the same sites being monitored by the Benthic Marine Communities, Marine Fish Communities, Freshwater Animal Communities (Streams and Anchialine Pools) monitoring protocols. This is a strategically planned component of the sampling design, specifically, using co-location to maximize comparison of interrelated monitoring datasets and integration of information across datasets (and vital signs) to form a holistic understanding of ecological condition over time. This information if utilized correctly will be more useful for management than separate individual monitoring results.

Various water quality studies are in progress, or are planned to assess conditions in or near the PACN parks. Some of these programs have been running for several years but very few are comprehensive in scope. Most study areas are outside of park boundaries and may have only one sampling location. Appendix I of the PACN monitoring plan (HaySmith et al. 2005) and Appendix F of this protocol list current and former water quality studies and monitoring projects that occurred within or immediately adjacent to park boundaries that included core water quality parameters identified in this protocol.

Federal, state, territorial, and commonwealth regulations on water quality standards provide a framework for designating and protecting water bodies for specific uses (Guam Environmental Protection Agency 2001, Commonwealth of the Northern Mariana Islands Department of Environmental Quality 2004, American Samoa Environmental Protection Agency 1999, State of Hawaii Department of Health 2004). In regards to the CWA Section 305(b), regulatory reporting to The United States Environmental Protection Agency (USEPA) by the territories and the State of Hawaii demonstrates an increase in the number of impaired water bodies as determined by local water quality standards for their respective designated uses. However, this indication of increasing impairments is potentially misleading as more water quality monitoring is taking place, and previously unmonitored and unlisted resources are being added to the CWA Section 303(d) list.

The parks of the PACN contain numerous pristine and unique water resources that are worthy of protection by designation as Outstanding Natural Resource Waters (ONRW). The USEPA recommends that states incorporate ONRW in their water quality standards. This legislative framework is absent from the state, territories, and commonwealth represented in PACN. Development of the NPS long term monitoring program in the PACN provides an opportunity to stimulate the use of ONRW designations in our region.

A successful monitoring program will be relevant to management questions that are consistent with the mission of NPS, its resource protection goals, and the enabling legislation for individual parks. Conversely, successful management of park water resources will rely heavily on the relevance of monitoring questions and resulting data.

1.6 Parks Where Protocol Will be Implemented
The water quality protocol is relevant to the following Pacific Island Network (PACN) National Park units: WAPA, AMME, NPSA, KALA, HALE, PUHE, KAHO, and PUHO. Portions of this protocol also may be used in collecting environmental information relative to other vital signs Monitoring in HAVO and ALKA. Funding may restrict implementation in parks without sufficient staff and/or to sites that are co-located with other protocols (e.g. freshwater communities). The guidance provided in this protocol will have sufficient detail to allow for the implementation of the sampling designs for the remaining PACN parks as funding becomes available. Methodologies developed in this protocol will be applicable to those eight PACN parks.

1.7 Vital Signs Objectives
In deciding priorities for vital signs, water quality ranked highest among all vital signs considered by the PACN and will contribute to six (Table 1) of the 31 general monitoring objectives for the Network outlined in chapter one of the PACN Monitoring Plan (HaySmith et al. 2006). To make this a successful monitoring program, it is being developed around specific questions and objectives, specifically to provide focus and clarity about the purpose and desired outcome of the monitoring program, and to be consistent and justifiable with current scientific knowledge (NPS 2006b).

Table 1. General monitoring objectives, and specific vital signs of the PACN I&M Program for which this water quality monitoring protocol will provide information to help interpret results and significance.

Level 1	Level 2	Vital Sign	Monitoring Objective
Water	Hydrology	Groundwater Dynamics	Determine aerial and vertical distribution of salinity levels in the PACN park units, ground-water levels in park units and surrounding areas, surface-water discharges from streams and springs, current and proposed distribution and rates of ground-water withdrawals in park units and surrounding areas, and effect of land-use changes on infiltration capacity and the recharge component of the water budget.
Water	Water Quality	Water Quality	Determine range, spatial variance, temporal trends, and spatial trends of temperature, pH, conductivity/salinity, dissolved oxygen (DO), total nitrogen (TN), total phosphorous (TP), nitrate (NO_3), turbidity, and chlorophyll in PACN surface water bodies (annually); and identify correlations between documented changes in land uses in watersheds.
Biological Integrity	Focal Communities	Freshwater Animal Communities	Determine trends in composition, diversity, distribution, and abundance of selected fish and invertebrates in selected freshwater and mixohaline communities, and improve understanding of relationships between freshwater animal communities and their habitat by correlating physical/chemical habitat measures with changes in distribution and abundance of fish and invertebrates.
Biological Integrity	Focal Communities	Benthic Marine Communities	Determine trends in abundance of sessile marine benthic invertebrate and algal assemblages stratified by habitat along a 10–20 m isobath; benthic small-scale topography stratified by habitat or reef zone; hard coral settlement rate on the fore reef along a 10–20 m isobath; growth and survival rates of randomly selected coral colonies of a common Pacific species found in all parks; and incidence and severity of coral and algal disease and bleaching.
Biological Integrity	Focal Communities	Marine Fish	Determine the density, distribution and biomass of visible diurnal reef fish assemblages in each park.
Geology and Soils	Soil Quality	Erosion and Deposition	Annually assess soil depth, quality (organic matter, pH, infiltration, aggregate stability, soil crusts), and loss/accretion at randomly selected monitoring sites stratified across rainfall and slope gradients in PACN parks; seasonally measure water column turbidity at marine and freshwater monitoring sites; and seasonally measure sediment collection rate and determine percent contribution & total load of terrestrial soils in marine and freshwater sediments.

1.8 Monitoring Objectives

Long-term monitoring is a repeated information-gathering effort to better understand how to track changes in ecosystems. Monitoring may serve as an "early warning system" to detect declining trends (as well as positive changes) in ecosystem integrity and species or population viability, ideally before irreversible change or loss occurs (Davis 1989; Wiersma 1984). The nature of the observed changes can guide managers to probable causes and suggest further investigations ultimately providing necessary information to support best management decisions and actions (White and Bratton 1980; Croze 1982; Jones 1986; Davis 1989; Quinn and van Riper 1990). In cases where natural systems in or near parks have been so highly altered that natural ecological processes no longer function properly, managers can use information from monitoring to understand how the altered systems operate, in order to determine the most effective approach(es) for restoration of systems and/or natural processes.

The overall goals of the National Park Service water quality monitoring are to gather data that will advance scientific understanding of Network water resources, inform management of water resource status relative to federal, state, and local water quality requirements, and to better inform resource management decisions. NPS management policies mandate that parks will determine the quality of their water resources, strive to avoid anthropogenic pollution occurring within and outside of park boundaries, and "perpetuate surface waters and groundwaters as integral components of park aquatic and terrestrial systems" (NPS 2006). Monitoring the quality of aquatic resources is an obligatory part of the NPS Inventory & Monitoring Program for the entire nation. The Pacific Island Network has developed this protocol to assess status and trends in freshwater, marine, and brackish water resources that include streams, wetlands, anchialine pools, and nearshore marine waters. Specifically, the water quality vital sign will address two monitoring questions with two overall objectives. These questions and objectives, with their justifications for selection, are as follows:

1.8.1 Monitoring Questions and Objectives to be Addressed by the Water Quality Protocol

Question 1: What are the ranges and variances of the network water quality parameters within selected water bodies?

- Objective 1: Determine the range and spatial variance on an annual basis of temperature, pH, conductivity/salinity, dissolved oxygen (DO), nitrate (NO_3), total nitrogen (TN), total phosphorous (TP), turbidity and chlorophyll in coastal marine waters, freshwater streams, wetlands, and anchialine pools, within eight PACN parks (WAPA, AMME, NPSA, KALA, HALE, PUHE, KAHO, and PUHO).

- Justification: The range of values and their variance for each parameter must be known for the appropriate water bodies (e.g. anchialine pools in KAHO) to assess water quality in parks. Pacific island water-resource types can exhibit a high degree of spatial variability, and the amount of sampling required to capture the variability and range must be determined. Therefore multiple samples and a review of existing data for these resources are necessary. In addition to the NPS core parameters, chlorophyll, turbidity, and nutrients are needed to evaluate water clarity and nutrification.

Question 2: What are the temporal and spatial trends of the network core water quality parameters for individual water bodies or water resource types in each park?

20

- Objective 2: Determine the temporal (events, diurnal, seasonal, annual, decadal) and spatial trends, for temperature, pH, conductivity/salinity, and dissolved oxygen in coastal marine waters, freshwater streams, wetlands, and anchialine pools, within eight PACN parks (WAPA, AMME, NPSA, KALA, HALE, PUHE, KAHO, and PUHO). If necessary, collect and analyze pilot field data to resolve knowledge gaps.

- Justification: In order to utilize water quality time series data to identify temporal and spatial trends, the variability for each parameter over time and space must be known. Range and variability of the water quality parameters may correlate with temporal patterns of drivers and stressors and therefore will be necessary to evaluate changes in other ecosystem components. Temporal trends will not be identified for all parameters at all scales, rather a subset will be identified based on known and expected parameter variability and relevance to resource condition.

2 - Sampling Design

2.1 Background

Many water quality monitoring protocols developed by various government agencies are readily available, but are not appropriate for detecting long term trends in the water bodies of the PACN. USEPA and the United States Geological Survey (USGS) are using well-tested methods to characterize water quality for various applications. The USEPA and many states and territories have also developed standards and recommendations for monitoring water quality from the standpoint of resource protection. These protocols are geared toward providing sampling strategies over a large spatial extent.

While these existing standards are valuable to their respective programs, the sampling designs are not suitable as they stand for the objectives of this protocol relative to the spatial extent in which we will be working; long term trends in aquatic resource condition for generally very small parks with multiple resource types in regions with differing water quality standards. A comprehensive review of these methods along with thorough testing and evaluation of sampling designs are necessary to achieve the program's goal of developing protocols that are adaptive, yet rigorous scientifically and statistically. Indeed, core aspects of existing protocols were used in developing this protocol.

Variability spatially and temporally is a confounding factor in water quality analyses, especially after exposure to catastrophic disturbance such as from a tropical cyclone. Given these conditions, a split panel sampling design allows for increased spatial sampling while simultaneously examining multiple temporal scales and permitting broader ecological and statistical inference beyond that provided by fixed or permanent sampling locations alone (Skalski 2005).

The purpose of this chapter is to outline the factors considered in selecting the sampling design, sampling frame, site selection and co-location, basic parameters, and frequency of collection. Based on various constraints including park size, available data, discussions with NPS and USGS scientists, PACN staff, and contract statisticians, the sampling design for the water quality vital sign monitoring will consist of 4 permanent (fixed) sampling station locations and 4 random non-fixed station locations that are not re-visited. The eight sampling stations will be sampled quarterly, and analyzed for the 10 objective parameters listed in the paragraph below. In addition, two extended deployment data sondes will be placed to collect physical water quality parameters (temperature, pH, DO, turbidity, chlorophyll, and conductivity/salinity) in each water resource type in each park. These sondes will be deployed for 3 month intervals logging once every hour (at a minimum) during both the rainy and dry season giving a total of 6 months of continuous diurnal physical water quality data at a minimum of two fixed sites within each park.

2.2 General Considerations

This protocol examines ten different parameters: water temperature, pH, salinity, conductivity, turbidity, dissolved oxygen (DO), chlorophyll, total phosphorous (TP), nitrate (NO_3), and total nitrogen (TN). These parameters vary across space and time, and as such, no single design can provide maximum statistical power for all ten parameters simultaneously. Therefore, the design was developed to maximize the statistical power of the NPS-WRD core parameters (temperature, pH, conductivity/salinity and DO) while providing information necessary for determining regulatory compliance (relative to federal, state, and/or territorial laws) as well as valuable information relevant to the interpretation and correlation of results to environmental factors affecting other aquatic vital signs biological monitoring efforts (Benthic Marine Communities, Marine Fish Communities, Freshwater Animal Communities: Streams, and Freshwater Animal Communities: Anchialine Pools). Statistical robustness and scientific rigor, however, are not the only criteria that need to be considered in the selection of the sampling design. Additional criteria include:

2.2.1 Maximizing Personnel Safety
Conducting monitoring work in the aquatic and marine environment presents special challenges and hazards. The safety of field personnel is a critical consideration in the site selection process. For example, sampling during high wave activity in the ocean, or sampling in narrow steep canyons during and immediately following rain events can be particularly hazardous.

2.2.2 Sample Number
The number of sampling stations was determined from both economical and statistical standpoints.

Additionally, given the financial resources of the PACN available to dedicate to water quality monitoring it was necessary to set sampling frequency to quarterly to maintain the WRD recommended minimum sample numbers, and still provide sufficient statistical power to obtain the spatio-temporal objectives outlined in chapter 1 of this protocol.

2.2.3 Spatial Coverage
Sampling requires sufficient spatial coverage throughout each park to provide broad inference beyond the sampling locations. The spatial coverage outlined in this design should be sufficient to make inferences to the entire target population within the sampling frame.

2.3.4 Logistical Constraints
Field activities such as site selection and sampling events are constrained by personnel and equipment availability, site location, topography, and weather. Thus, each park has a limited window of time when field activities can be conducted, restricting the number of sites that can be completed within the sampling design.

2.3.5 Fiscal Constraints
Collecting quarterly water quality samples in the freshwater, brackish, and marine environments across the PACN is expensive, requiring specialized equipment and trained staff. Fiscal constraints within this program affect the availability of sampling equipment and staffing levels, as well as the frequency and number of monitoring locations that can be visited. To keep within the budget, primary field work (sonde operations, site selection, data collection, and sample filtering) for this protocol will be conducted by trained in-park and PACN personnel with secondary assistance from volunteers, other park staff, and/or scientists in training (college or university students).

2.3.6 State, Territorial, and Commonwealth Water Quality Compliance Criteria

Water quality compliance criteria differ between parks throughout the PACN (Appendix H). These differences occur not only in the acceptable levels or changes in water quality parameters, but also in the parameters being measured. Because most of the Parks are located within the state of Hawaii, and park GPRA goals for water quality are only explicitly stated in the strategic plans of Hawaii parks, the state of Hawaii water quality monitoring criteria were selected as the target criteria to use when designing the monitoring.

2.3.7 Integration with Other Vital Signs

To enhance the value of the datasets collected, the water quality protocol was designed to be integrated with all of the other aquatic Vital signs protocols in the PACN (marine benthic communities, marine fish communities, freshwater stream communities, and groundwater). This design includes co-locating and co-visiting during identical sampling periods for marine benthic communities, marine fish communities, freshwater stream communities, and freshwater anchialine pool communities vital signs monitoring, and was established to lend greater correlative power to the aquatic vital signs utilizing the environmental variables monitored in this protocol. In addition, this also provides an economical benefit, reducing the total sampling costs recognized by the PACN during these sampling overlaps.

2.4 Basic Parameters

2.4.1 Target Population

The target population for this protocol is defined as: Safely accessible selected aquatic resources located within PACN park boundaries. Selected aquatic resources include: perennial freshwater streams, nearshore coastal marine areas, and brackish water –anchialine pools with the exception of PUHE. Safely accessible perennial streams are limited in their upper reach by the presence of cliffs/waterfalls that cannot be navigated around without considerable threat to safety. Safely accessible marine areas include nearshore coastal sites with sufficient water depth to allow a sampling event to occur from a vessel without power outside of any wave break zone. Safely accessible brackish water includes all brackish and hyper-saline water that can be safely navigated to without the use of rappelling equipment. This means that inferences based on this protocol can be made to the target population defined above.

This protocol should, at a minimum, be able to identify frequency and degree to which monitored water quality parameters in the target population exceed the minimum and maximum thresholds of local governmental water quality standards, in addition to providing the parks with the answers to the objectives outlined in Chapter 1 of the protocol narrative (i.e. seasonal trends in selected water quality parameters).

2.4.2 Sampling Frame

The marine sampling frame includes all safely accessible marine waters within park boundaries (e.g., Figure 10). The freshwater sampling frame is comprised of the all waters within the total safely accessible length of perennial streams located within park jurisdictional boundaries. The brackish water sampling frame includes all safely accessible anchialine pools and hyper-saline water bodies located within park boundaries. It is necessary to limit the water quality monitoring to these sampling areas for safety, logistical, and economic reasons. The sampling frames for each all PACN parks are available in Appendix D along with graphical representations of sampling site locations.

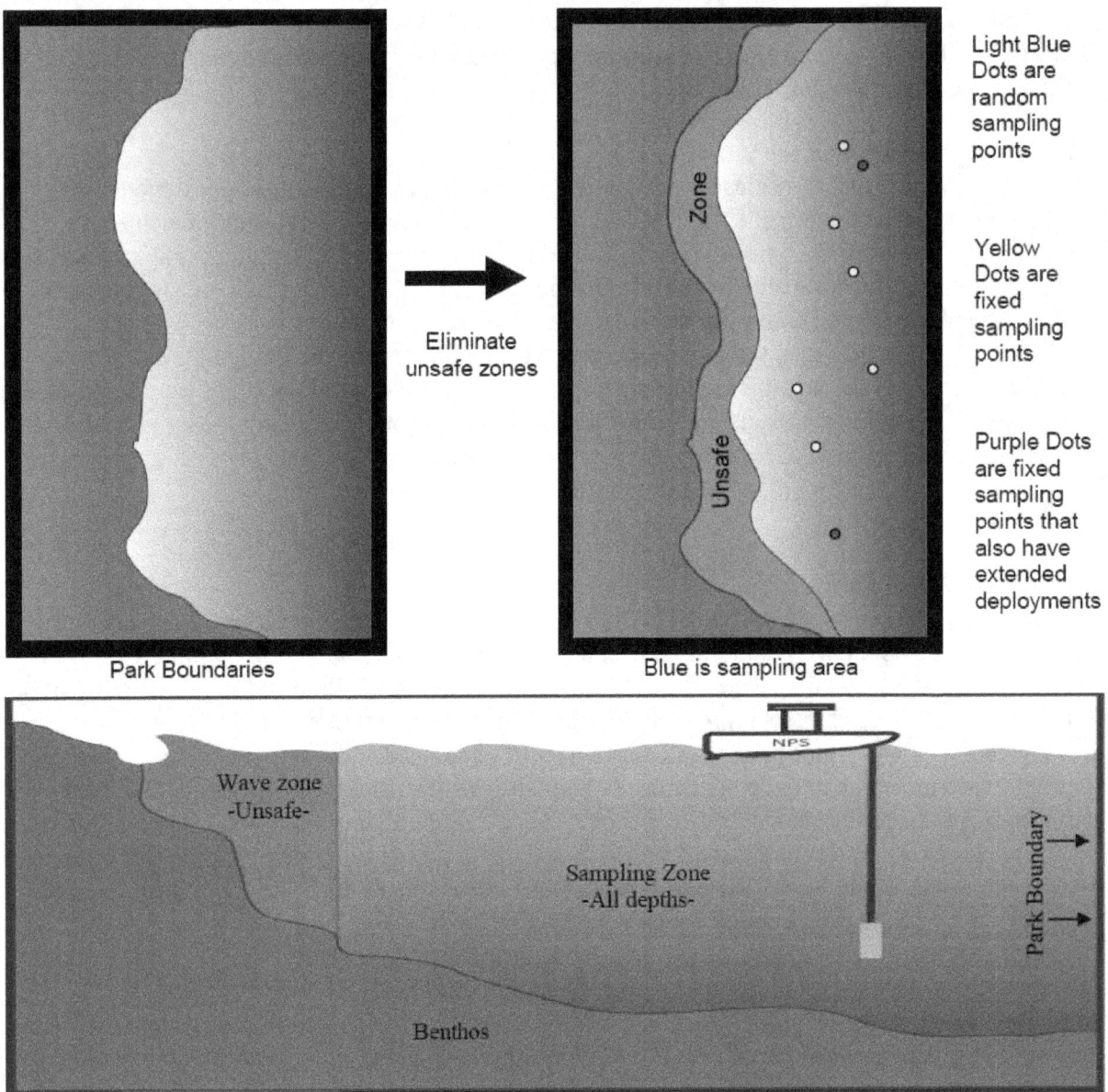

Figure 10. Generalized sampling frame representations for safely accessible marine waters showing park boundaries, sample sites, and unsafe areas.

2.4.3 Representativeness

The sampling design incorporated by the PACN includes a design of randomly chosen fixed and variable station locations that should represent a spatially unbiased characterization of the daytime water quality parameters of monitored water bodies of the PACN. In addition, some fixed locations will be placed near the mouths of streams to assess the total load of measured parameters that stream delivers/removes to/from the ecosystem for compliance and environmental correlative purposes. These characterizations represent a complete daytime census every three months, of the water resources in AMME, PUHE, and PUHO.

In addition, this sampling design should give a spatially unbiased accurate daytime representation of the water quality of marine waters in WAPA, KALA, NPSA, and KAHO as well as the anchialine pools in KAHO, and the lower reaches of freshwater streams in NPSA, KALA, and HALE. The statistical robustness of this design should be sufficient to make a statistically sound determination of the water quality compliance criteria outlined by state, federal, territorial, and commonwealth governments for measured parameters for each park in addition to informing park resource managers of both the status and trend of their water quality resource.

Furthermore, this monitoring design uses extended deployment continuously monitoring sondes. The use of these sondes will yield seasonal and diurnal representations of resource status in the immediate vicinity of the aquatic resource in which they are placed. An additional benefit of using continuously logging sondes at fixed sampling sites is that the data collected from the sondes at each quarterly sampling event will provide for the possibility of extending deployed data sampling inference to the rest of the sampled water body over time by creating a statistically robust correlation between continuous samples and other fixed sampling sites point sampled at the same time as continuous sampling occurs. While it will take time and repeated samples to generate a robust statistical correlation, once that correlation is developed, continuous sondes will yield representations through inference of the entire resource in which they are placed.

2.4.4 Sampling Units
The fundamental sampling unit for monitoring the water quality vital sign is a sample station. A sample station is defined as a single point in the water resource which is large enough to accommodate collection of water samples and deployment of the instrumentation. This unit should provide adequate characterization of the freshwater, marine, and brackish resources of the PACN parks.

Standard methodologies and equipment will be used to collect data in each sampling unit through the use of multiparameter sondes with pH, temperature/conductivity, optical dissolved oxygen, optical turbidity, and optical chlorophyll probes and a field water filtering apparatus. The sampling design will incorporate this equipment using the standard methodology designed for each water quality monitoring apparatus as defined in the respective user manual. For a more detailed account of these methodologies, see SOP 7 (Conducting Water Quality Sampling).

2.5 Statistical Evaluation of Existing Data Sets

2.5.1 Annual Precision
Precision in estimating variables is affected by multiple sources of variation, including spatial, temporal, and analytical. Increasing precision is obtained by increasing replication within the largest component of variation. Equation 2.1 shows precision of the estimate (E) as a function of variability in the sample design. Precision in estimating water quality parameters is affected by three sources of variability:

at the level of site: Coefficient of Variation$_1$ (CV_1)

at the level of sampling station within a site: Coefficient of Variation$_2$ (CV_2)
at the level of measurement error (analytical): Coefficient of Variation$_3$ (CV_3)

Annual precision is estimated using Equation 1.

$$E = Z_{1-\alpha/2}\sqrt{\frac{(1-f_1)CV_1^2}{n} + \frac{(1-f_2)CV_2^2}{nm} + \frac{(1-f_3)CV_3^2}{nmk}}$$ (Equation 1)

Where:

f_1 = fraction of area sampled by sites (Assume that $1-f_1 = 1$)
f_2 = fraction of area sampled by sampling stations within a site (Assume that $1-f_2 = 1$)
f_3 = fraction of area sampled by transects repeated for measurement error (Assume that $1-f_3 = 1$)

n = number of sites
m = number of sampling stations per site
k = number of samples repeated for measurement error
and,
$Z_{1-\alpha/2}$ = distribution value for selected confidence interval

2.5.2 Existing Estimates of Expected Variation
Variability of water quality fluctuates temporally and spatially (Tables 2 and 3) and is highest (e.g., variance to mean ratio of 3–4) when storm events occur. This is due to the sudden nature and inconsistent spatial impact of these events on aquatic resources. Precision is increased by maximizing replication at the level of park (n).

For the purposes of this protocol we used:

$Z_{1-\alpha/2}$ = 1.96 = distribution value for "95% of the time"
$n = 8$ = number of sites within a resource
$m = 1$ = number of sampling stations within a site
$k = 3$ = number of samples repeated for measurement error

28

Table 2. Cyclical variation of network core parameters for water quality may occur daily, seasonally, episodically, or due to anthropogenic influences. The following table uses water quality results gathered from various sources collecting water quality data in the region.

			Marine								Stream				
Park	Max	Min	Mean	Var	Cv	n	Prcsn	Park	Max	Min	Mean	Var	Cv	n	Prcsn
Temp (°C)															
WAPA	32.1	24.8	28.5	2.1	0.05	191	± 0.72%	WAPA	31.9	4.2	27.4	6.6	0.09	436	± 0.88%
AMME	34.1	23.1	28.5	3.5	0.07	372	± 0.67%	NPSA	26.4	23.4	25.1	0.53	0.03	21	± 1.24%
NPSA	29.8	26	28.1	3.9	0.07	4	± 6.89%	KALA	23	14.5	19.5	2	0.07	313	± 0.8%
								HALE	26	15.5	20.5	3.2	0.09	238	± 1.11%
Turbidity (NTU)															
WAPA	62	0.1	2.8	37.3	2.18	200	± 30.23%	WAPA	98	0.23	7.7	247	2.04	249	± 25.25%
AMME	110	0.2	5.1	53.8	1.44	652	± 11.04%	NPSA	13	0.1	2.7	9.7	1.15	21	± 49.34%
NPSA	1.5	-0.8	0.2	1.4	5.92	4	± 579.78%	HALE	8	0	1.9	4.7	1.20	12	± 68.15%
pH															
WAPA	9.1	6.9	7.9	0.07	0.03	172	± 0.5%	WAPA	8.6	1	7.9	0.29	0.07	226	± 0.89%
AMME	8.7	5	8.1	0.05	0.03	652	± 0.21%	NPSA	8.1	7.5	7.8	0.04	0.03	21	± 1.1%
NPSA	8.2	8	8.1	0.01	0.01	4	± 1.21%	KALA	9.3	5.8	7.3	0.34	0.08	137	± 1.34%
								HALE	8.8	4.27	6.6	0.54	0.11	257	± 1.36%
Salinity (ppt)															
WAPA	35	1.4	32.9	25	0.15	177	± 2.24%	NPSA	0.09	0	0.06	8E-04	0.46	21	± 19.65%
AMME	42	12	31.9	8.6	0.09	582	± 0.75%								
NPSA	37	16.1	32.8	37.5	0.19	11	± 11.03%								
DO (mg/L)															
WAPA	9.7	2.3	6.2	1.9	0.22	197	± 3.02%	WAPA	12.2	2.2	7.3	2	0.19	351	± 2.03%
								NPSA	8.5	7	7.9	0.2	0.06	18	± 2.62%
								KALA	9.4	9	9.2	0.03	0.02	5	± 1.65%
								HALE	12.2	3.4	8.3	1.6	0.15	200	± 2.11%
DO(%sat)															
WAPA	128	30.3	79.2	334	0.23	187	± 3.31%	WAPA	153	42.2	90.6	298	0.19	319	± 2.09%
AMME	238	27.8	95.6	629	0.26	337	± 2.8%	NPSA	104	84.3	95.8	24.3	0.05	15	± 2.6%
NPSA	87.5	82.7	85.1	11.5	0.04	2	± 5.52%	HALE	140	37.8	91.3	190	0.15	206	± 2.06%
TN (μg/L)															
WAPA	720	0	21.6	3598	2.78	185	± 10.02%	WAPA	325	0	27.5	2258	1.73	298	± 19.62%
AMME	58.7	8.48	25.9	0	0.00	30	± 0.02%	NPSA	431	0	101.6	5041	0.70	38	± 22.22%
NPSA	93.3	11.7	24.4	924	1.25	7	± 92.29%								
Chl a															
NPSA	0.6	-0.5	0.17	0.09	1.76	9	± 115.29%	NPSA	0.47	0.09	0.26	0.015	0.47	11	± 27.84%
Sp. Cond (mS/cm)															
NPSA	55.5	26.3	44.3	196	0.32	4	± 30.97%	NPSA	0.19	0.11	0.15	6E-04	0.16	21	± 6.69%
								KALA	126	47	103.1	322	0.17	138	± 2.9%
								HALE	52	15	33.2	90.4	0.29	64	± 7.02%

29

Table 3. Coastal and anchialine pool precision estimates for water quality parameters based on 10 years of data from NELHA (1996–2005). The year 2004 was used as the yearly precision estimator because that is the last full year of data available.

Statistic	NO$_3$ (μM)	TDP (μM)	TDN (μM)	Turbidity (NTU)	Salinity (o/oo)	Temp/F (Deg C)	pH	DO (ppm)	Chl a (μg/L)
Coastal									
2004									
Mean	9.82	0.65	19.11	0.27	31.96	26.24	8.26	7.08	0.18
Variance	521.17	0.28	690.70	0.02	22.05	1.32	0.00	0.30	0.02
CV	2.32	0.81	1.38	0.51	0.15	0.04	0.01	0.08	0.74
Count	44	36	36	44	44	44	44	28	32
Precision	± 69.3%	± 26.5%	± 45.0%	± 17.3%	± 4.4%	± 1.4%	± 0.20%	± 3.3%	± 27.7%
10 year									
Mean	9.49	0.73	19.93	0.17	32.27	25.65	8.25	7.21	0.21
Variance	521.43	0.48	868.37	0.01	32.76	2.01	0.01	0.28	0.04
CV	2.41	0.96	1.48	0.65	0.18	0.06	0.01	0.07	0.93
Count	341	209	209	345	308	348	345	201	198
Precision	± 25.6%	± 13%	± 20.1%	± 6.9%	± 2.0%	± 0.6%	± 0.1%	± 1.0%	± 13%
Anchialine									
2004									
Mean	100.96	3.39	110.47	0.22	10.34	22.33	7.88	7.38	0.22
Variance	733.44	0.04	900.14	0.02	3.05	0.89	0.03	1.27	0.07
CV	0.27	0.06	0.27	0.71	0.17	0.04	0.02	0.15	1.21
Count	8	8	8	8	8	8	8	8	8
Precision	± 20.2%	± 5.2%	± 22.4%	± 52.4%	± 11.9%	± 3.2%	± 1.6%	± 11.5%	± 87.9%
10 year									
Mean	88.45	3.46	96.55	0.33	10.01	22.85	7.90	7.97	0.69
Variance	1155.21	0.25	964.55	0.18	5.81	3.51	0.04	3.81	2.48
CV	0.38	0.14	0.32	1.31	0.24	0.08	0.03	0.25	2.29
Count	77	76	77	78	72	82	78	78	74
Precision	± 8.7%	± 3.3%	± 7.3%	± 29.2%	± 5.6%	± 1.9%	± 0.6%	± 5.6%	± 52.5%

Illustrated in Tables 2 and 3 is the increasing precision with increasing sample size. The annual sample size for point samples at most parks is estimated to be approximately 32 samples (8 samples per park multiplied by 4 sampling periods per year). Taking into account the relative similarity between the one and 10 year means and CVs, regardless of the sample size, we see increasing sample size increases precision significantly. Using the current protocol sample sizes (32 per year), we can expect a precision of the parameter estimates to be similar to the precision estimates seen in Table 3.

These sample sizes are based on what I&M and the parks can feasibly survey under logistical and financial constraints. Using Equation 1, the CV values from Tables 2 and 3, and the sample size estimate of 32, the annual relative precision 95% of the time for measured water quality parameters are shown in Table 4.

Water quality is highly variable spatially and temporally. For instance, nitrate (NO_3) levels can vary by one to two orders of magnitude at a temporal scale of one month within a given site. Levels can vary spatially by two to three times. Numerous factors influence water quality parameters (e.g., nutrient loading, water motion, biota, toxic chemicals, storm events, geology, and erosion). As a result, variation in water quality parameters is not completely understood. The variance to mean ratio for samples at a site is often greater than one.

Table 4. Estimated annual relative precision based on the sampling regime outline in this protocol using an *n* of 32.

	Coastal		Anchialine		Streams	
Parameter	CV	Precision	CV	Precision	CV	Precision
NO3 (µM)	2.41	± 18.15%	0.38	± 0.45%	Need more data	
TDP (µM)	0.96	± 2.88%	0.14	± 0.06%	Need more data	
TDN (µM)	1.48	± 6.85%	0.32	± 0.32%	1.73	± 9.35%
TURBIDITY (NTU)	0.65	± 1.32%	1.31	± 5.36%	2.04	± 13.01%
SALINITY (o/oo)	0.18	± 0.10%	0.24	± 0.18%	0.46	± 0.66%
TEMP/F (Deg C)	0.06	± 0.01%	0.08	± 0.02%	0.09	± 0.03%
pH	0.01	± 0.00%	0.03	± 0.00%	0.11	± 0.04%
DO (ppm)	0.07	± 0.02%	0.25	± 0.20%	0.19	± 0.11%
Chl a (µg/L)	0.93	± 2.70%	2.29	± 16.39%	0.47	± 0.69%

2.5.3 Proportion of Fixed Versus Random Panels (Transects)
The goal of this monitoring effort is to detect change over time with sufficient statistical power. The split panel design selected for this protocol maximizes the spatial replication while reducing the within site effort using a combination of fixed and rotating panels to maximize power. The optimal proportion of fixed to rotating panels can be estimated from the correlation (r) between years within sites (Equation 2).

$$\text{Proportion of fixed to random sites} = \frac{\sqrt{1-r^2}}{1+\sqrt{1-r^2}} \qquad \text{(Equation 2)}$$

With greater correlation between months, fewer fixed panels are needed. Some water quality parameters at sites are highly correlated from month to month, ranging from 0.64 to 0.94 (Table 5) resulting in a fixed:random panel ratio of 26% to 43%. However, other water quality parameters, have lower inter-monthly correlations of 0.10 to 0.32 resulting in a proportion of fixed to random sites between 49% and 50% (data obtained from KAHO water quality sampling project 2004–2006, Bienfang 2006). Therefore, a conservative design has been selected in which 50% of the panels are fixed and the remaining, rotating panels are visited only once before replacement.

Table 5. Monthly correlations (*r*) of water quality parameters at KAHO and NPSA sampling sites in 2005. Data obtained from Kaloko-Honokohau water quality sampling (Bienfang 2006) and National Park of American Samoa (unpublished data).

Parameter	*r*	Panel Fraction	Park
Temperature	0.32	0.49	NPSA
DO	0.67	0.43	NPSA
Turbidity	0.17	0.50	NPSA
Salinity	0.10	0.50	NPSA
pH	0.64	0.43	NPSA
Chlorophyll	0.66	0.43	KAHO
Nitrate	0.94	0.26	KAHO
Phosphorus	0.92	0.29	KAHO

2.5.4 Statistical Power Estimation

When determining the power to detect change over time it is important to consider several characteristics of water quality data (Helsel and Hirsch 2002): distributions (can be skewed or normal), outliers, cycles (diurnal, seasonal, etc.), missing values, censored (below MDLs), and serial correlations. It is important to choose methods that are robust enough to handle all characteristics of water quality data. Often the most effective methods for parameters that are notoriously variable (i.e. turbidity, chemistry, oxygen) and often non-normally distributed are non-parametric methods. This protocol measures multiple variables at multiple sites and as such, the USGS recommends the use of non-parametric methods for analyses (Helsel and Hirsch 2002).

This protocol intends to use the methods of analyses as outlined by the USGS in the Statistical Methods for Water Resources (Hlesel and Hirsch 2002). The initial trend methods recommended in this protocol for detecting a trend are the Sen slope estimator and the seasonal Kendall trend test. These methods can handle missing and non-normal data. While similar in approach, the trend slope estimator will give an estimate of the slope of temporal data by comparing every month against every other month, ranking the results, and taking the median as the trend slope estimate (McBride 2005). This can be compared with the Kendall trend test which is slightly more sophisticated, taking the differences in all years and months, replacing values with normalized change indicators (+ slope gets a 1, no slope gets a 0, and - slope gets a -1), computing the year weighted variance for each month, then computing the test statistic for that variance. The answer will give a trend with a significance *p*-value (McBride 2005, Helsel and Hirsch 2002). Using these two tests is a powerful method of determining if there is a trend (increasing or decreasing) present in the water quality data and whether that trend is significant. However, they do not detect specific changes (i.e. 25% decrease in nitrate).

Parametric methods give you the ability to detect a specific change with a specific confidence over a specified timeframe but are much more rigid in their requirements and often take longer and require more samples to get statistically significant results. However, using these parametric statistical methods can often be useful when trying to understanding variability and difficulty detecting trends in environmental samples as well as for determining sample sizes (Irwin 2008). Using parametric methods, analyses of the available data was calculated based on the sample size in this protocol. Because of the necessity for high sample sizes to achieve high powers to

32

detect change, logistical constraints, including staffing and budget considerations were the primary determinants of sample size (Tables 6 and 7).

The sample size estimations and power results were determined using two methods: a paired t-test analysis using an online calculator (SS Twosamples at statsalive.com) recommended by WRD (Irwin 2008) and by a sample size independent power calculator (variance is the primary driver: if increased sample sizes decrease variance, the power increases but *a priori* knowledge of the change in variance with sample size is not required) created by a statistician hired by the PACN network to consult on statistical sampling designs for monitoring protocols (Skalski 2005). The t-test was good at estimating the sample sizes and power, but lacked an ability to test for a specific change (i.e. β). Based on the variability associated with annual analyses from previous work, the Skalski methods appeared more appropriate and conservative.

The results of the marine water analyses are seen in Tables 6 and 7. Based on the Skalski and statsalive.com results, using sample sizes of 4 with variances noted in Table 3, marine water samples outlined in this protocol are sufficient to have, using an $\alpha = .10$, a minimum of 21% chance of detecting a 25% change in chlorophyll over 10 years or alternatively a 45% power to detect differences in the mean using a t-test. There was an 88% chance of detecting a 25% change in DO over 10 years or alternatively a 100% power to detect differences in the mean using a t-test. An 11% chance of detecting a 25% change in NO_3 over 10 years or alternatively a 33% power to detect differences in the mean using a t-test was indicated. A 99% chance of detecting a 25% change in pH over 10 years or a 100% power to detect differences in the mean using a t-test was discovered. Also, a 35% chance of detecting a 25% change in salinity 10 years or a 100% power to detect differences in the mean using a t-test was seen. The results also showed a 21% chance of detecting a 25% change in TDP over 10 years, or a 90% power to detect differences in the mean using a t-test as well as a 96% chance of detecting a 25% change in temperature over 10 years or a 100% power to detect differences in the mean using a t-test. Finally, a 12% chance of detecting a 25% change in turbidity over 10 years or 43% power to detect differences in the mean using a t-test was shown (Tables 6 and 7).

These powers to detect change were calculated assuming fixed sampling stations each quarter. Note the relatively low power estimated on the highly variable parameters of nitrate, chlorophyll, TDP, and turbidity using the Skalski approach (Table 6). It is interesting to note that while salinity in the marine environment is relatively stable, the Skalski calculations show a low power to detect change. This quandary arises from the data used. In this set of calculations, data were collected relatively nearshore in Hawaii bringing higher variability associated with groundwater flow runoff into the nearshore marine environment. After five years of data have been collected within the parks using the protocol methodology it will be important to revisit the power to detect change calculations to determine more correctly the actual power to detect change given this sampling design and using real data from the parks. We are confident that eight sampling stations per quarter with four fixed can be surveyed with the current staff and resources of the I&M PACN and its parks.

The results of the anchialine pool analyses are seen in Tables 6 and 7 and were similar to marine water. Based on the Skalski and statsalive.com results, using sample sizes of 4 with variances noted in Table 4, anchialine pool samples outlined in this protocol are sufficient to have, using an

$\alpha = .10$, a minimum of 9% chance of detecting a 25% change in chlorophyll over 10 years or alternatively a 26% power to detect differences in the mean using a t-test. There was a 30% chance of detecting a 25% change in DO over 10 years or alternatively a 100% power to detect differences in the mean using a t-test. A 24% chance of detecting a 25% change in NO_3 over 10 years or alternatively a 100% power to detect differences in the mean using a t-test was indicated. A 99% chance of detecting a 25% change in pH over 10 years or a 100% power to detect differences in the mean using a t-test was discovered. Also, a 30% chance of detecting a 25% change in salinity 10 years or a 100% power to detect differences in the mean using a t-test was seen. The results also showed a 48% chance of detecting a 25% change in TDP over 10 years, or a 100% power to detect differences in the mean using a t-test as well as an 81% chance of detecting a 25% change in temperature over 10 years or a 100% power to detect differences in the mean using a t-test. Finally, a 12% chance of detecting a 25% change in turbidity over 10 years or 33% power to detect differences in the mean using a t-test was shown (Tables 6 and 7). This power was calculated assuming fixed sampling stations each quarter. We are confident that eight sampling stations per month can be surveyed with the current I&M and park staff and resources.

Parametric statistical power is expected to be higher than represented in the previous paragraphs for most water quality parameters in the proposed design, taking advantage of the statistical power benefits of the panel sampling strategy. Because 50% of the sample sites will be re-surveyed annually, this will allow for the refinement of parameter estimates using multiple years of data (e.g., increased parameter precision). These methods have been used to significantly increase statistical power in other monitoring programs (Skalski 2005). After five years of data have been collected within the parks using this design, it will be important to revisit the parametric power to detect change calculations to determine more correctly the actual power to detect change given this sampling design and using real data from the parks.

In addition, the powers presented are for detecting annual changes in water quality parameters for which variability is high, reducing the power to detect change. However, the power to detect change on a seasonal basis should be considerably higher than examining parameters on an annual basis. Nevertheless, this represents the minimum power of this design. The true power of this design will need to be revisited after three to five years of consecutive sampling, and the sample sizes adjusted accordingly. Regardless, non-parametric methods can be used to determine if there is an increasing or decreasing trend in any monitored water quality parameter sooner than parametric methods. Thereby, allowing management to be informed of resource trend and alerting them to the need of possible action.

Table 6. Statistical power for a one-tailed F distribution at $\alpha = 0.05$ and $\alpha = 0.10$ for detecting relative changes of 10%, 25%, and 50% in selected water quality parameters in anchialine pools and marine sites. Values were calculated using data collected by NELHA water quality monitoring between 1993 and 2005. The detection level selected for this protocol is highlighted in bold (

Marine Sites

	Power Output Chl a Relative Change		Power Output DO Relative Change		Power Output pH Relative Change		Power Output NO3 Relative Change	
$\alpha=0.05$	5 yrs	10 yrs	5 yrs	10 yrs	5 yrs	10 yrs	5 yrs	10 yrs
10%	0.046	0.059	0.169	0.249	0.999	0.999	0.017	0.022
25%	0.103	0.107	0.471	0.763	0.999	0.999	0.043	0.055
50%	0.111	0.124	0.913	0.999	0.999	0.999	0.086	0.104
$\alpha=0.10$								
10%	0.091	0.117	0.305	0.395	0.999	0.999	0.034	0.044
25%	0.204	0.209	0.674	0.878	0.999	0.999	0.085	0.109
50%	0.217	0.233	0.981	0.999	0.999	0.999	0.171	0.205

Anchialine Pools

	Power Output Chl a Relative Change		Power Output DO Relative Change		Power Output NO3 Relative Change		Power Output pH Relative Change	
$\alpha=0.05$	5 yrs	10 yrs	5 yrs	10 yrs	5 yrs	10 yrs	5 yrs	10 yrs
10%	0.014	0.019	0.106	0.113	0.095	0.104	0.475	0.767
25%	0.036	0.046	0.135	0.176	0.112	0.125	0.999	0.999
50%	0.072	0.093	0.235	0.384	0.146	0.199	0.999	0.999
$\alpha=0.10$								
10%	0.029	0.037	0.210	0.218	0.189	0.206	0.678	0.880
25%	0.072	0.092	0.254	0.304	0.219	0.235	0.999	0.999
50%	0.144	0.184	0.397	0.548	0.270	0.333	0.999	0.999

35

Table 6. Statistical power for a one-tailed F distribution at $\alpha = 0.05$ and $\alpha = 0.10$ for detecting relative changes of 10%, 25%, and 50% in selected water quality parameters in anchialine pools and marine sites. Values were calculated using data collected by NELHA water quality monitoring between 1993 and 2005. The detection level selected for this protocol is highlighted in bold (continued).

Marine Sites

Relative Change	Power Output Salinity 5 yrs	Power Output Salinity 10 yrs	Power Output TDP 5 yrs	Power Output TDP 10 yrs	Power Output Temp 5 yrs	Power Output Temp 10 yrs	Power Output Turbidity 5 yrs	Power Output Turbidity 10 yrs
$\alpha = 0.05$								
10%	0.108	0.119	0.042	0.054	0.205	0.323	0.019	0.024
25%	0.152	0.214	0.102	0.106	0.612	0.897	0.047	0.061
50%	0.297	0.512	0.109	0.120	0.999	0.999	0.095	0.104
$\alpha = 0.10$								
10%	0.213	0.227	0.083	0.107	0.356	0.482	0.038	0.048
25%	0.280	0.352	0.204	0.208	0.804	0.958	0.094	0.121
50%	0.478	0.666	0.214	0.228	0.999	0.999	0.189	0.206

Anchialine Pools

Relative Change	Power Output TDP 5 yrs	Power Output TDP 10 yrs	Power Output Salinity 5 yrs	Power Output Salinity 10 yrs	Power Output Temp 5 yrs	Power Output Temp 10 yrs	Power Output Turbidity 5 yrs	Power Output Turbidity 10 yrs
$\alpha = 0.05$								
10%	0.117	0.137	0.106	0.112	0.156	0.220	0.032	0.041
25%	0.202	0.318	0.134	0.173	0.408	0.679	0.080	0.103
50%	0.459	0.750	0.230	0.373	0.857	0.999	0.106	0.111
$\alpha = 0.10$								
10%	0.227	0.252	0.209	0.217	0.285	0.360	0.064	0.081
25%	0.352	0.476	0.252	0.300	0.609	0.816	0.159	0.204
50%	0.663	0.869	0.390	0.537	0.960	0.999	0.209	0.216

Table 7. Sample size and power output of *t*-test calculations based on WRD recommended online calculator (SS Two samples from statsalive.com). Blue are coastal sites, red are anchialine pools, and yellow are stream sites (based on NPSA 2005 and NELHA 2004 data). Fixed sites were calculated as paired samples while mixes of random and fixed sites calculated as same sample size, independent samples; *r* values were taken from Table 5. Fixed and annual fixed are representative of the protocol, while mixed fixed and random columns represent the *t*-test output using pooled fixed and mixed site data treated as independent equal sample size comparisons. The last two pairs of columns (excluding the r column) represent paired and independent (respectively) high power *t*-test values and their associated sample sizes.

Parameter	Fixed Samples (4 samples)	Power	Fixed & Random Samples (8 samples)	Power	Annual Fixed (16 Samples)	Power	Annual Fixed & Random (32 samples)	Power	Number of Fixed Samples (n)	Power	Number of Random Samples (n)	Power	r
NO3	4	16%	8	8%	16	33%	32	11%	65	80%	393	45%	0.94
TDP	4	37%	8	15%	16	90%	32	34%	32	100%	380	100%	0.92
TDN	4	25%	8	10%	16	65%	32	18%	66	100%	370	80%	0.94
Turbidity	4	19%	8	24%	16	43%	32	61%	129	100%	154	100%	0.17
Salinity	4	66%	8	95%	16	100%	32	100%	13	100%	13	100%	0.1
Temperature	4	100%	8	100%	16	100%	32	100%	3	100%	3	100%	0.32
pH	4	100%	8	100%	16	100%	32	100%	2	100%	2	100%	0.32
DO	4	100%	8	100%	16	100%	32	100%	3	100%	5	100%	0.67
Chl a	4	19%	8	16%	16	45%	32	36%	119	100%	346	100%	0.66
NO3	4	99%	8	56%	16	100%	32	98%	5	100%	42	100%	0.94
TDP	4	100%	8	100%	16	100%	32	100%	3	100%	3	100%	0.92
TDN	4	99%	8	55%	16	100%	32	98%	5	100%	43	100%	0.94
Turbidity	4	16%	8	19%	16	33%	32	47%	193	100%	232	100%	0.17
Salinity	4	56%	8	88%	16	100%	32	100%	16	100%	17	100%	0.1
Temperature	4	100%	8	100%	16	100%	32	100%	3	100%	3	100%	0.32
pH	4	100%	8	100%	16	100%	32	100%	2	100%	2	100%	0.32
DO	4	93%	8	93%	16	100%	32	100%	6	100%	15	100%	0.67
Chl a	4	15%	8	11%	16	26%	32	21%	94	80%	273	80%	0.66
Sp. Cond.	4	72%	8	97%	16	100%	32	100%	11	100%	11	100%	0.1
TDN	4	53%	8	18%	16	99%	32	41%	18	100%	279	100%	0.94
Turbidity	4	9%	8	7%	16	8%	32	9%	321	25%	377	25%	0.17
Salinity	4	19%	8	25%	16	42%	32	67%	130	100%	144	100%	0.1
Temperature	4	100%	8	100%	16	100%	32	100%	3	100%	2	100%	0.32
pH	4	100%	8	100%	16	100%	32	100%	3	100%	2	100%	0.32
DO (%sat)	4	100%	8	100%	16	100%	32	100%	3	100%	3	100%	0.67
DO (mg/L)	4	100%	8	100%	16	100%	32	100%	3	100%	3	100%	0.67
Chl a	4	32%	8	28%	16	81%	32	69%	43	100%	123	100%	0.66
T-test treatment	Paired		Independent, Equal		Paired		Independent, Equal		Paired		Independent, Equal		

It is also important to note the results of Table 7, as this was instrumental in determining effective sample sizes and the protocol design. Using random sites allows status to be determined, a primary objective of the protocol. However, the question of trend still needed to be addressed. Initial consultations with statisticians leaned toward a design using both random and fixed sites, with the fixed aimed at determining trend with the random aimed at status. Examining these results confirmed the initial direction of the protocol design. Using random sites (the last paired column in Table 2.6), it is clear that the number of samples needed for the majority of the parameters being measured to determine even a difference in mean (let alone determining trend), far exceeded the possibilities of sampling effort reasonably available.

Furthermore, the results from table 7 indicate that a relatively small number of fixed sites was necessary to get relatively high power in several of the monitored parameters, yielding only a few parameters with relatively low powers to detect differences in the mean. These hard to detect differences parameters were problems in each water resource (turbidity, and chlorophyll) and required significant numbers of fixed sites that were beyond the reasonable expectations of effort and budget. This focused the design on statistically more manageable parameters, and the target detection levels.

2.6 Targeted Detection Level
Based on the analysis of the existing data sets and incorporating logistical and fiscal constraints, the targeted detection level for water quality measurements is ±50% of the baseline mean for each individual monitoring parameter, expressed as a relative measurement of change. For example, in regions where a baseline parameter is 0.65 μM, our target detection level is ± .32 μM change in absolute value (50% relative). Regardless; however, this protocol is also designed to deter mine if park waters exceed applicable water quality standards. As such, a minimum detection level of applicable standard criteria values (Appendix H) is required of all analyses.

2.7 Rationale for Sampling Design
Several different spatial and temporal sampling designs were considered for this protocol. Spatial designs included simple random sample, systematic sample (grid), stratified random sample, cluster sample, and Generalized Random Tessellation Stratified (GRTS) (DeBacker et al. 2005). Each of these spatial designs has advantages and disadvantages. The PACN water quality protocol has chosen the simple random sample in water resources for the following reasons:

1. This is the simplest strategy to setup and implement within a Geographic Information System (GIS).

2. This strategy ensures that every portion of the sampling frame has an equal probability of being selected. Many of the PACN parks have water quality parameters that are relatively unknown (e.g., KALA); therefore it would be difficult to stratify or cluster sampling units based on known habitats, geomorphological structures, or organism distribution patterns.

3. The GRTS system, while appealing, is complicated to implement without contracted statisticians (DeBacker et al. 2005). Limited resources within the PACN preclude use of this approach.

Temporal designs considered in this protocol included sites always revisited, sites never revisited, rotating panels with sites sampled on x consecutive occasions, and split panels which partitions sites into two or more revisit designs (McDonald 2003). Again, each approach has strengths and weaknesses. The PACN water quality protocol has selected the split panel design for the following reasons:

1. A split panel sampling design allows for increased spatial sampling while simultaneously examining multiple temporal scales and permitting broader ecological and statistical inference beyond that provided by fixed or permanent sampling locations alone (Skalski 2005).

2. The split panel design maximizes the spatial replication while reducing the within site effort using a combination of fixed and rotating panels to maximize power.

3. Sampling a new set of sites annually minimizes the bias in estimates of status and continually updates prior estimates through time series calculations (Skalski 1990).

4. Leaving fixed sites within the design is useful for several reasons. First, the majority of the historical data uses fixed sampling locations (USGS) so spatial comparisons will be simpler. Second, after the initial random setup, the fixed transects should be easier to resample, thus reducing preparation time and ultimately costs to generate the random grid for subsequent transect measurements (Green and Smith 1997). Third, utilizing exclusively randomized sampling without fixed sites makes it difficult to detect change in water quality parameters if change occurs dramatically over time; random design measures inherent spatial variation at each sampling period, which adds variance associated with spatial heterogeneity rather than changes or patterns that are time-related (Green and Smith 1997). Fourth, fixed sites can provide additional information in variance structure that is difficult to obtain with random transects [e.g., (Connell et al. 1997)]. Finally, interpreting results from fixed sites is much easier for the general public and resource managers to comprehend than using a straight randomized sampling design.

In essence, the split panel sampling strategy will give the PACN both status and trend, spatially and temporally, with historical comparability. This fits the objectives stated in chapter 1 perfectly, while other sampling designs would need either significant modification or the use of more than one design to address both status and trend both spatially and temporally.

2.8 Establishing Sampling Stations (Spatial Design)

2.8.1 Sample Site Selection Process

To determine the location of the sampling units for monitoring, spatial coordinates for potential sampling stations will be randomly generated *a priori* in a GIS program (e.g., ArcInfo 9.1) using habitat characterization maps. Sampling sites must be accessible, and water resources large/deep enough to sample. With the exception of a few select fixed sampling stations, both fixed and random sites will be determined randomly. Select fixed sites will be established at the mouth of each stream in the sampling frame to assess the total outflow of the river into the surrounding environment.

Sample unit selection will continue until enough (4) fixed sites meeting the criteria have been selected. Randomly selected alternative locations will also be generated in case the initial locations are unsuitable with respect to safety, accessibility, or resource availability (ie. adequate pool size). Full details can be found in SOP 6 (Selecting Water Quality Sampling Stations) and in a brief narrative provided below.

In addition to the sampling stations selected for fixed sites, each quarter, 4 random sampling station locations (plus 4 additional alternative coordinates) will be generated and sampled. These points will follow the same selection criteria as outlined above. If the generated random points have been used previously for either fixed or random transects then an alternative transect location will be used (unless all possible sampling locations have previously been sampled, i.e. limited numbers of anchialine pools). When all sites are selected, they should be arranged in proximal order to minimize travel time and prevent contamination of the water resource at other sampling locations.

Before starting field work, the site coordinates and station ID numbers should be entered into a Global Positioning System (GPS); see SOP 4 (Using GARMIN Global Positioning System [GPS] Units). In addition, station ID numbers should be added into the handheld datalogger devices for each piece of sampling equipment (SOP 7). Fixed sites should have the letter F as a prefix to the station ID number. Random sites should have the letter R as a prefix to the station ID number.

2.9 Sampling Frequency (Temporal Design) Panel Description

In the PACN, catastrophic infrequent events, such as tropical typhoons, can cause significant disturbances in water quality. However, sampling all sites in all water resource types would greatly limit the sample numbers, and hence the level of spatial coverage, and the breadth of ecological and statistical inference that could be achieved. A split panel design will allow monitoring on a monthly basis while maximizing spatial sampling and the breadth of inference by increasing the number of sites monitored. For example, after the first year of monitoring eight sites quarterly with 4 permanent sites and a second set of 4 randomly determined rotating sites, the total number of distinct sites surveyed would be 20 and 52 after the third year (Table 8). Rotating panels will generally not be revisited (except for the limited number of anchialine pools), but all sampling sites for water quality will be co-located in the same sampling frame with protocols for monitoring marine fish, benthic marine communities, and freshwater animal communities.

Sampling size is partly based on current staffing and fiscal constraints (see above). At the present time, PACN park staff can sample up to eight sites quarterly in each of the PACN parks. This level of replication will be evaluated as data are collected in the 3–5 years following implementation of the monitoring program and modified as needed.

The current sampling design is based on consideration of safety issues, logistical limitations, financial constraints, analyses of sample data sets for the principal monitoring parameters, and consultations among statisticians and experienced Aquatic Ecologists. The PACN parks; however, currently lack adequate water quality data to provide spatial and temporal variation within each park. This information is necessary to develop a final sampling design. This requires collecting, analyzing, and interpreting several years of data. The design for this monitoring plan has been developed with the best available data, but it is anticipated that modifications within an adaptive sampling design framework will be necessary as implementation proceeds. It is critical to this monitoring program that the data be collected and analyzed annually, and that the results be used to adaptively "fine-tune" the design to optimize effort, statistical power, and inference. It is anticipated that the statistical power of this design will increase the values estimated here.

Table 8. Theoretical one year panel survey schedule for the mixed panel design with 4 permanent/fixed panels and 4 rotating panels. Green indicates year 1; purple, year 2; and orange, year 3.

Panel	Jan	Apr	Jul	Oct	Jan	Apr	Jul	Oct	Jan	Apr	Jul	Oct
							Month					
1–4	X	X	X	X	X	X	X	X	X	X	X	X
5–8	X											
9–12		X										
13–16			X									
17–20				X								
21–24					X							
25–28						X						
29–32							X					
33–36								X				
37–40									X			
41–44										X		
45–48											X	
49–52												X

3 - Field Methods

The ability to reliably detect differences in resources over time or among sites is only assured if data are gathered in a consistent and well-documented manner (Beard et al. 1999). The field methods section is intended to ensure consistent methodology and repeatability in light of changing personnel (Beard et al. 1999). Those aspects of field methodology that are repeated in different locations and/or by different personnel will be written in the form of a standard operating procedure (SOP). SOPs are detailed written instructions intended to ensure uniformity and consistency of a given procedure within the protocol. SOPs need to be easy to read and implement. For more information on specific field details, please see the appropriate SOP.

3.1 Field Preparations, Field Schedule and Equipment Setup

Before entering the field, personnel should review this entire protocol, including all of the SOPs and recommended references listed at the end of this document. The staff should pay special attention to the tasks described in SOP 1 (Before the Field Preparations) and SOP 2 (Training Technicians). Equipment and supplies listed in SOP 1 should be organized and made ready for the field, and copies of the field data forms found in Appendix E should be made on waterproof paper.

Sampling dates and personnel should be scheduled and logistics should be organized no later than three months in advance to allow for individual parks to accommodate sampling necessities. However, flexibility is needed in scheduling sampling trips because of unpredictable weather, oceanic conditions, and staff workloads. Please see SOP 1 for details on chronological logistics.

3.2 Conducting the Field Sampling

3.2.1 General Sampling Strategy

The water quality monitoring strategy consists of quarterly sampling (once every three months) in eight PACN parks. Sampling will target three water resource types: perennial freshwater streams, nearshore coastal marine, and brackish (generally anchialine pools with the exception of PUHE). Not all parks possess each of the three aquatic environments; therefore, sampling intensity will vary by park. Sampling will be conducted only in weather conditions that are safe for field work. Freshwater monitoring will focus on perennial streams and will be limited to safely accessible reaches. Selection of marine sampling locations may also be limited; contingent upon on shoreline, current, and weather conditions. Anchialine pools will be the primary type of brackish water resource monitored.

The sampling strategy is comprised of a three-pronged approach, outlined in Figure 11 (see below.) For specifics of conducting sampling at each sampling site see SOP 7.

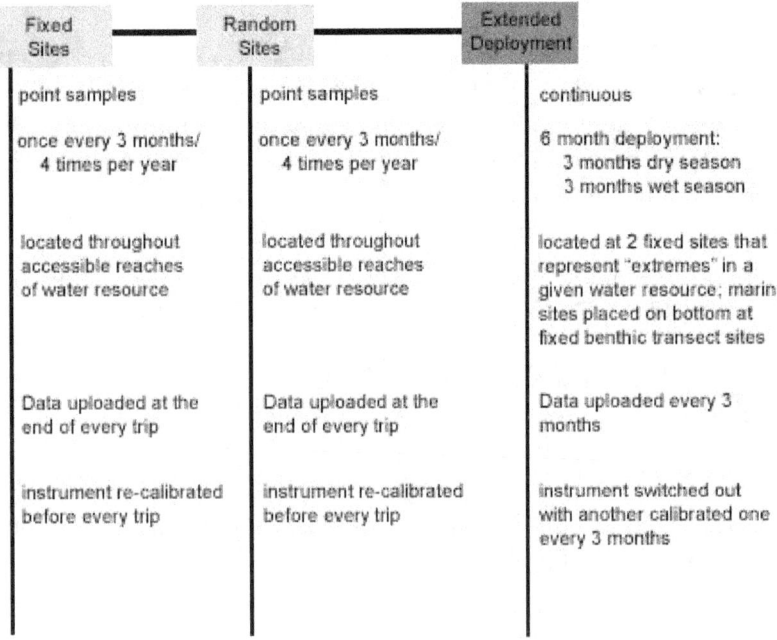

Figure 11. PACN Inventory & Monitoring Program's three-pronged approach to water quality vital sign monitoring.

1) Quarterly random point sampling

- Random points will be chosen to compliment fixed sites within each park, one random site for each fixed site.

- Random points will be generated for sampling in fresh, marine, and brackish water to evaluate the current status of each water resource.

- Random sites in marine waters will be co-located with random sites for the benthic marine community and marine fish monitoring at the time of the year in which those protocol sampling events coincide (co-visitation of benthic marine community and marine fish monitoring will occur once annually in NPSA, WAPA, KALA, and KAHO, see Table 9).

- Random sites in the freshwater environment will be co-located with the random sites for the freshwater animal community monitoring when protocol sampling events coincide (co-visitation of the freshwater animal community monitoring will occur once annually in NPSA, WAPA, KALA, and HALE).

- Co-location will add environmental correlates to the interpretation and analyses of the other vital signs monitoring results.

- When co-visitation occurs, water quality will always be taken prior to sampling for other monitoring protocols to avoid potential contamination of the sample.

- Random point sampling will collect pH, temperature, dissolved oxygen (DO), chlorophyll, turbidity, and salinity/conductivity data using a multiparameter sonde.

- Water samples will be collected in 125mL bottles. Samples will be field filtered using a syringe filter, kept on ice until return to the office, then frozen, and sent to the lab for nutrient analysis as soon as possible (total phosphorous (TP), total nitrogen (TN) and nitrates [NO_3]).

- Digital pictures of each sampling site will be taken to document the environmental conditions present at the time of sample collection.

Table 9. PACN Inventory & Monitoring Program's Current Proposed Aquatic Sampling schedule in relation to Water Quality Vital signs monitoring.

Protocol Month	Water Quality	Freshwater Animals	Groundwater	Benthic Marine	Marine Fish	Anchialine Pools
January	NPSA, WAPA, AMME		AMME	WAPA	WAPA	
February	KAHO, ALKA, PUHO, PUHE		KAHO			PUHO
March	HALE, KALA		AMME			
April	NPSA, WAPA, AMME	WAPA	KAHO	NPSA	NPSA	
May	KAHO, ALKA, PUHO, PUHE		AMME			HAVO
June	HALE, KALA	HALE	KAHO	KALA	KALA	
July	NPSA, WAPA, AMME	NPSA	AMME			
August	KAHO, ALKA, PUHO, PUHE		KAHO			KAHO
September	HALE, KALA	KALA	AMME			
October	NPSA, WAPA, AMME		KAHO			
November	KAHO, ALKA, PUHO, PUHE		AMME	KAHO	KAHO	PUHE
December	HALE, KALA		KAHO			

2) Quarterly fixed site sampling

- Fixed sites throughout the varying water resource types will be generated before protocol monitoring implementation, then visited each sampling trip.

- Fixed sites are established by recorded GPS locations, navigation directions, site descriptions, and site images, all determined on the initial visit. No permanent markers will be established beyond directions and site identification descriptions. Anomalies in the site from the previous descriptions will be noted and the appropriate changes made to the directions for the next sampling period.

- Fixed site samples will be used to determine the trends in quality of the water resource.

- Fixed sites in marine waters will be randomly identified and co-located with the randomly selected fixed benthic marine community and marine fish sampling sites to add environmental correlates when interpreting and describing the benthic resource monitoring results.

- Fixed sites in the freshwater environment will be randomly determined and co-located with fixed sites for the freshwater animal community sampling.

- When co-visitation occurs, water quality will always be taken prior to sampling for other monitoring protocols to avoid potential contamination of the sample.

- Fixed point sampling will collect pH, temperature, DO, chlorophyll, turbidity, and salinity/conductivity using a multiparameter sonde.

- Water samples will be collected in 125mL bottles. Grab samples will be field filtered with a syringe filter, kept cold or frozen, and sent to the lab for nutrient analysis (total phosphorous [TP], total nitrogen [TN] and total nitrates [NO_3]).

- Digital pictures of each sampling site will be taken to document the environmental conditions present at the time of sample collection.

3) Extended deployment of water sampling instrumentation.

- Extended deployment sondes will be placed at fixed locations that represent extremes in the given water resource type (i.e. lower and upper reaches of a stream).

- A multiparameter probe will be utilized to collect pH, temperature, DO, chlorophyll, turbidity, and salinity/conductivity measurements.

- Deployment will occur six months a year in three months intervals; one in the dry season and one in the wet season. Sondes will be rotated or removed and information will be collected during quarterly sampling trips.

- Calibrations will take place prior to and following deployments to determine instrument sensor drift.

- Continuous and point sampling will occur simultaneously, to provide a quality control comparison between the instruments.

- The extended deployment comparison data will be particularly useful in understanding the variation of physical water quality parameters along the lengths of streams.

3.2.2 Park Specific Sampling

The basic monitoring strategy will be refined by park based on the existing water resources in each park (Table 10) and the logistical complexities associated with conducting sampling. Sample site locations for initial implementation are seen in Appendix D.

Table 10. Quarterly sampling strategy for all PACN parks each quarter, including measurement parameters and total number of samples at each site.

	Number of Samples			
Parks	**Streams**	**Pools**	**Marine**	**Measurement Parameters**
AMME	0	8	0	Total Nitrogen
WAPA	8	0	8	Total Phosphorous
NPSA	8	0	8	Total Nitrate
KALA	8	0	8	Dissolved Oxygen
HALE	10	0	0	Turbidity
ALKA	0	8	0	pH
PUHE	0	3	0	Temperature
KAHO	0	8	8	Salinity
PUHO	0	7	0	Conductivity
HAVO	0	8*	0	Chlorophyll
Total	**34**	**42**	**32**	**10 Parameters**

*HAVO pools are monitored annually.

WAPA: Sampling will take place in Asan Stream, one of two perennial streams in WAPA. The other perennial stream (Namo) has only approximately 100 meters of total reach within the park and was therefore determined to not be advantageous to monitor give limited resources. There are marine components in the Agat and Asan units. No known brackish water resources are present in WAPA. Water sampling will follow the general sampling strategy outlined in the protocol and occur quarterly (≈16 samples quarterly, field effort: four days).

AMME: This unit contains a short ephemeral stream that was constructed to receive runoff from the city of Garapan and a small wetland. Monitoring the wetland and this drainage will require eight samples quarterly due to the small size of these resources. The limited aquatic resources allow for a complete census of AMME resources, and the small park size allows for relatively quick and easy access to all areas of the park (≈8 samples quarterly, field effort: one day).

NPSA: Fixed and random sites will be sampled quarterly for both freshwater streams and nearshore marine waters on each of the park's three island units (Tutuila, Ofu, and Tau). All units include marine waters, but no known brackish resources. Tutuila and Tau both contain perennial streams. Significant topographical relief presents challenging logistical issues in sampling the streams on Tutuila and Tau. (≈16 samples quarterly, field effort: 6 days)

- Freshwater Sampling: On Tutuila, freshwater sites will be restricted to the lower reaches of Fagatuitui and Vatia streams because of steep terrain and waterfalls (≈4 samples, field effort: one day). Freshwater monitoring on Tau will focus on accessible reaches of the only perennial stream, Laufuti (≈4 samples quarterly, field effort: two days). There are no freshwater resources within park boundaries on Ofu.

- Marine Sampling: Marine areas on Tutuila and Ofu will be limited to safely accessible marine waters located within park boundaries. Marine waters of Tau will not be monitored until a safe and reliable method of collecting samples can be arranged. (≈8 samples quarterly, field effort: two days).

KALA: All three water resource types exist in this park. Freshwater sampling will focus on Waikolu Stream, the sole perennial stream in the park. The marine areas are relatively extensive and extend the length of the park. Freshwater sampling will occur in the same month as the marine monitoring efforts (≈16 samples quarterly, field effort: five days).

HALE: Only freshwater resources exist within the boundaries of this park; primarily in the Kipahulu region. A significant portion of the freshwater resources are inaccessible and therefore not possible to monitor. Monitoring will focus on the accessible lower reaches of Palikea, the largest perennial freshwater stream in the park, its tributary (Pipiwai Stream), and Alelele stream. Palikea Stream is relatively long, and some upper reaches may be accessed through the Kipahulu Biological Reserve (≈8 samples quarterly, field effort: five days per month).

ALKA: Currently, the undefined linear boundaries of ALKA preclude establishing specific water quality monitoring by the NPS Inventory and Monitoring program except in known alignment locations. A portion of the coastal watersheds of west Hawaii are currently being monitored by various groups and agencies. The Aquatic Ecologist will primarily rely on this monitoring data when reporting on the status of the trail. Additional water quality data will be available from NPS I&M monitoring conducted within the four PACN parks traversed by ALKA (PUHE, KAHO, PUHO, and HAVO). The water quality monitoring efforts conducted through I&M will supplement known activities as deemed appropriate by agreement between I&M and the ALKA superintendent (≈8 samples quarterly, field effort: three days).

PUHE: There are no perennial streams or marine areas within the boundaries of this park. There is an ephemeral hyper-saline brackish water body which will be monitored quarterly. This will constitute a complete census of the park aquatic resources (≈3 samples quarterly, field effort: one day).

KAHO: There are no streams within or near KAHO, but there is a significant marine and brackish component. Marine and brackish waters (anchialine pools) will be sampled quarterly following the general sampling strategy (≈16 samples quarterly, field effort: two days).

PUHO: There are no perennial streams or marine areas within the boundaries of PUHO. Several anchialine pools (estimated 13) exist in this park. This park has easy access to both the water resources and the park itself (quarterly sampling ≈7, field effort: one day)

HAVO: There are no perennial streams or marine areas within the boundaries of HAVO. Anchialine pools (approximately 28 known pools) are the sole aquatic resource in this park. These pools are located in remote locations along the eastern HAVO coastline and require significant time and effort to sample. However, because of the logistical difficulty in accessing these sites, these sites will only be monitored once annually while the Freshwater Animal Communities: Anchialine Pools Vital signs monitoring takes place in those same locations ($\approx$8 samples annually, field effort: six days).

3.2.3 Options
With supplementary funds, time, and personnel, additional monitoring could be conducted to strengthen the water quality dataset. Recommended additions to the monitoring protocol are listed.

Options include:

- Sampling additional sites in KAHO anchialine pools
- More fixed and random sampling sites in NPSA streams
- Deployment of miniature 12-bit temperature data loggers at marine fixed transects sites and random marine sites within all marine parks.
- Water level loggers placed at fixed water quality site locations, as well as continuous deployment sites in anchialine pools and streams
- Sampling additional sites in KAHO fishponds.
- Marine depth profiles for physical parameters at fixed (or all) sites.

3.2.4 Chronological Integration of Surveys
The proposed design requires fixed sampling locations along with an equal number of random sites in each of the eight quarterly sampled parks; the number of sampling sites is park-specific. New random sites will be generated before each sampling trip and fixed sampling sites need to be established during the initial implementation of the protocol. The time required to sample a monitoring site will depend on the difficulty arriving at each site. A full complement of sampling components at an individual site should take approximately 30 minutes for a team of two. When sampling is co-located with another Vital signs protocol, water quality sampling at that site will always take place prior to the start of the other protocol sampling. A minimum of two personnel are required to conduct sampling for safety purposes.

3.2.5 Process of Sampling
Water quality sampling should be conducted in such a manner that continuous data is collected concurrently with point samples. Collecting constant with quarterly fixed site data provides a calibration control and will aid in the interpretation of inconsistencies. At locations where extended deployment sondes will be placed, deploy before taking any point samples.

To conduct a sampling event at any site, site selections must be made (SOP 6). Marine field sites will be accessed by boat while land field sites will be accessed by hiking. For detailed directions to field sites consult SOP 6. On the day of the field work, at the office, an initial calibration of the instruments must be conducted (for explicit details on calibration, see SOP 5. Pre-sampling Equipment Preparation). Calibration is to include a second check of the sensor and a record of the variation from the calibration standard in the calibration notebook. In addition, ensure appropriate field gear is worn, a sufficient number of sample bottles are present, bottle labels and permanent markers are available, batteries have enough charge to conduct a day of monitoring, back-up batteries are available, and data sheets and field notebooks with appropriate writing utensils are present. A safety plan is then filed with the appropriate park identifying individuals present, contact information, emergency contact names, emergency contact information, site locations, route of travel, expected time of departure and expected return time. If feasible the safety plan should also include check in times. Selected sites are then navigated to using a GPS unit (SOP 4) and other necessary means (boat, car, feet, helicopter). Once a monitoring site is reached, the process for conducting sampling at an individual site begins (see SOP 7 for complete details).

- Freshwater Sampling Process (Figure 12): Approach the site from downstream moving upstream, taking care not to disturb or contaminate upstream waters. Using three random number pairs, find the exact sampling locations. This should be done by creating a coordinate system where x is the total distance across the stream in percentages (0 is the bank you are on and 100 is the opposite bank). Looking upstream, y extends 10 meters. The three random number pairs are then used as a percentage for x and a distance in meters upstream for y. If any location falls on a rock outcropping or other unsampleable area, an alternate coordinate is used. Once locations are determined, they should then be approached from downstream so as not to contaminate other water sampling locations (i.e. work upstream). Syringes are used to collect water for filtering and sample bottle rinsing. Sample bottles are washed three times with filtered site water then filled with filtered site water. The sample bottles are then filled with filtered site water and stored on ice. The multiparameter sonde is then set up and placed just upstream of the water sample collection sites in a representative part of the stream and set to log every 30 seconds (a minimum of 5 minutes, or 10 points, of data are collected). Pictures are then taken of the site and the environmental data sheets are filled in.

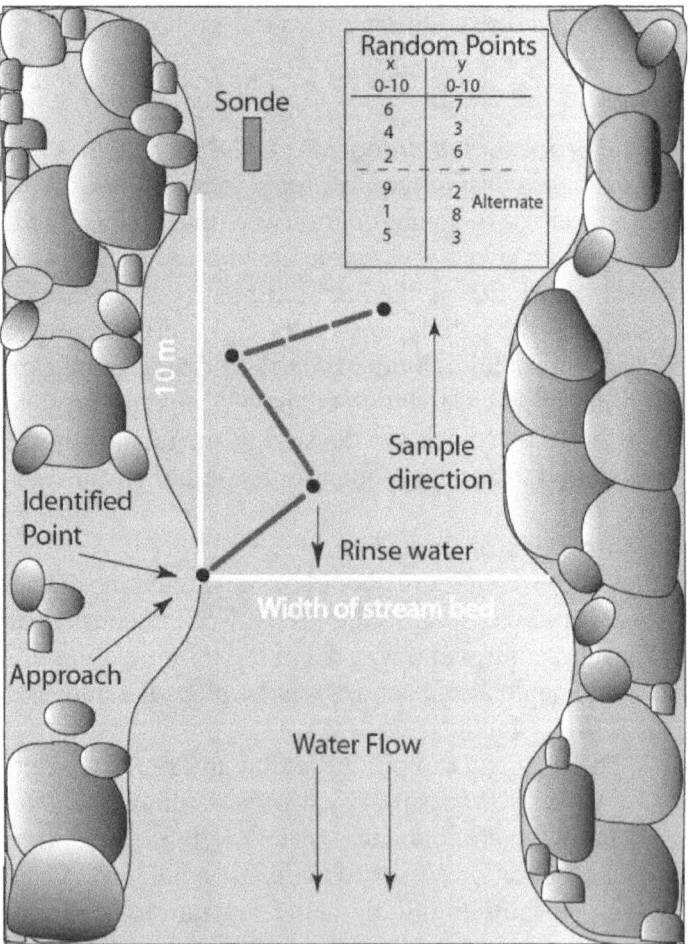

- Marine Sampling Process (Figure 13): Once the boat

Figure 12. Freshwater sampling process.

reaches a location, the engines are turned off and a niskin sampler is dropped to the afore identified depth and a sample is collected. This water is used to fill a syringe and rinse a bottle three times. The sample bottles are then filled with filtered site water and stored on ice. This entire process is repeated three times to collect real replicates (filtering three samples from the same niskin draw is not acceptable). The sonde is then lowered to the randomly selected depth and data is collected for a minimum of 5 minutes at 30 second intervals. (Optional: At fixed sites, the sonde is lowered at 1 meter intervals for 1 minute at each depth with the data set to record every 5 seconds to collect a complete depth profile for the site first). Meanwhile the data sheet is filled out and above water site location images are taken (i.e. facing shore). Once the sonde has finished collecting the requisite minimum 10 samples, a snorkeler takes a minimum of one underwater site photo of the sample location.

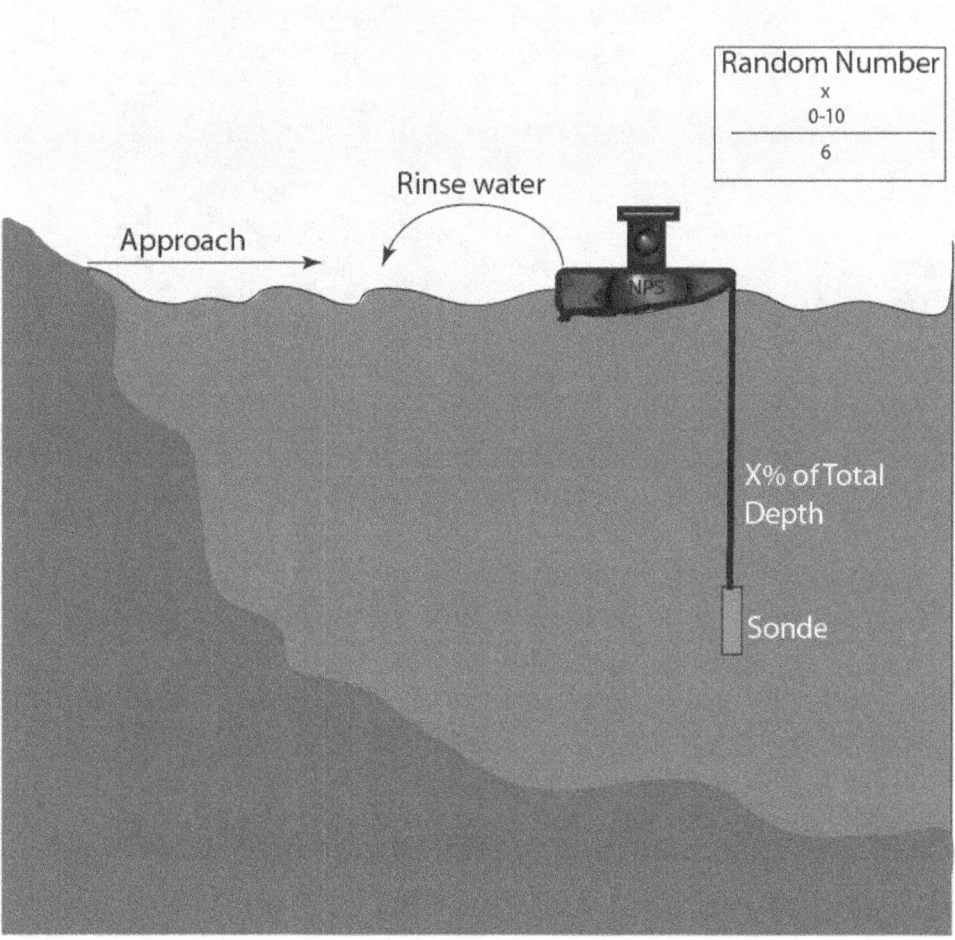

Figure 13. Marine sampling process.

- Anchialine Pool Sampling Process (Figure 14): Syringes are used to collect water for filtering and sample bottle rinsing. Sample bottles are washed three times with filtered site water. The rinse water is dumped away from the anchialine pool so as not to contaminate the water. Sample bottles are then filled with filtered site water taken from the center surface waters of the pool. Three replicate water samples are taken at each site and placed in an ice filled container. The multiparameter sonde is then set up and placed in the pool at the surface as close to the top layer as possible and set to log every 30 seconds (a minimum of 5 minutes, or 10 points, of data are collected). Please note, you may need to hold the instrument in place. Pictures are then taken of the site and the environmental data sheets are filled in.

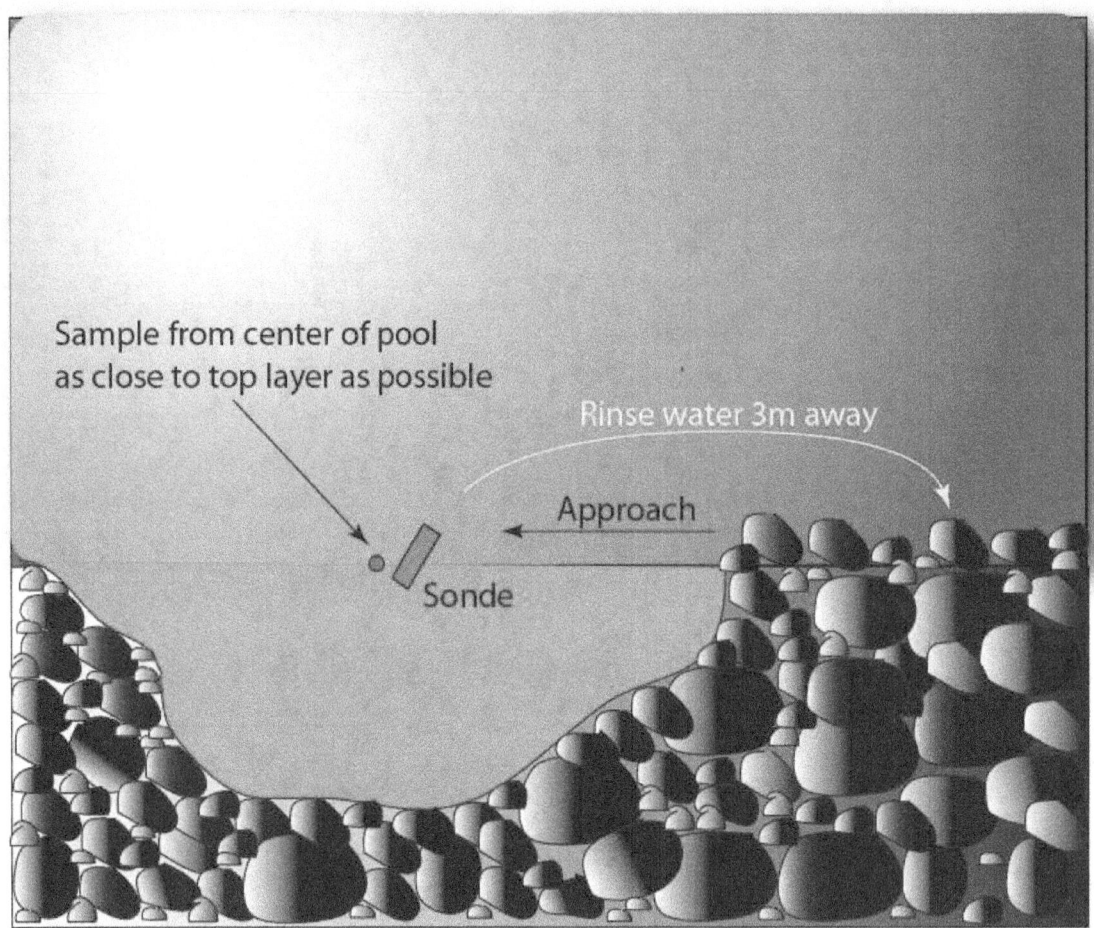

Figure 14. Anchialine pool sampling process.

- Wetland Sampling Process (Figure 15): Locate the random sampling site locations. This should be done by creating a coordinate system where x and y extend 10 meters from your location into the wetland. The three random number pairs are then used as a coordinates in meters for x and y. If any location falls on a rock outcropping, tree, or other unsampleable area, an alternate coordinate is used. Approach the site so as to disturb the wetland as little as possible. Sample bottles are washed three times with filtered site water. The rinse water is dumped away from the anchialine pool so as not to contaminate the water. Three replicate water samples are taken at each site and placed in an ice filled container. Three replicate water samples are taken at each site and placed in an ice filled container. The multiparameter sonde is then set up and placed in the wetland slightly away from the area of disturbed water and set to log every 30 seconds (a minimum of 5 minutes, or 10 points, of data are collected). Pictures are then taken of the site and the environmental data sheets are filled in.

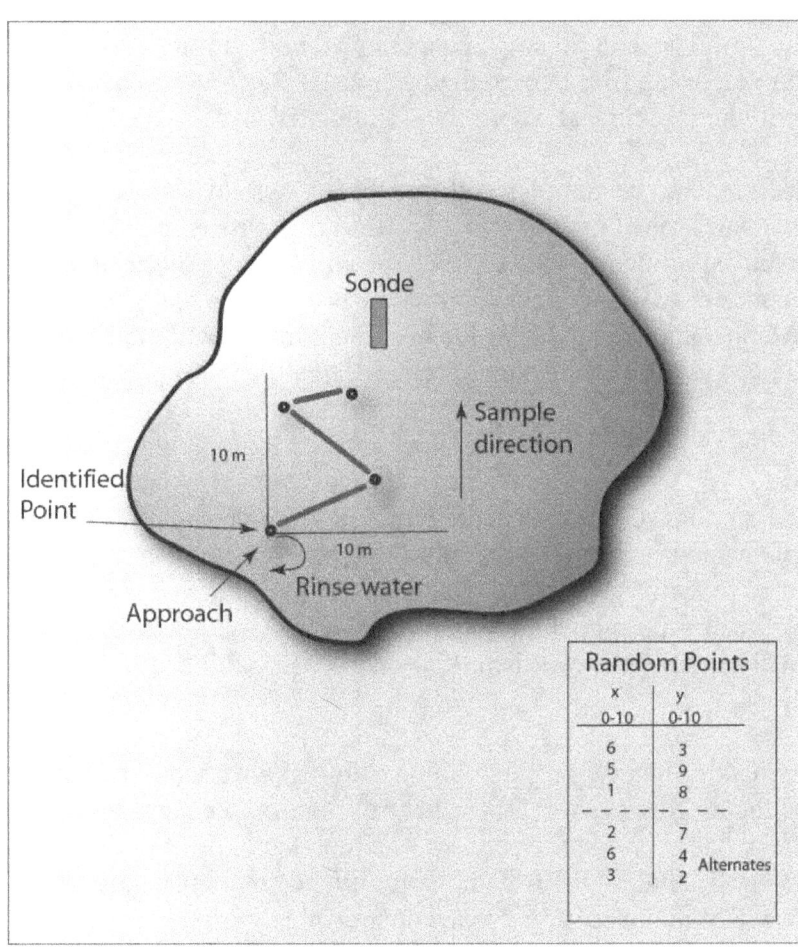

Figure 15. Wetland sampling process.

3.3 After the Field Procedures

Following return from the field, water samples will be immediately placed in a freezer. The samples will be sent to the appropriate lab as soon as possible (within 48 hours) using next day postal service or hand deliver, taking care to keep the samples in as close to a frozen state as possible. Along with the samples, a minimum of one blind blank and known blind standard should be sent in the same type sample bottles for lab QC. If the lab fails QC checks more than two times, a new lab will be sought. The lab will then process the samples for TP, TN, and NO_3 (details of current selected lab and analyses are found in SOP 9. Quality Assurance Project Plan). The variance in the replicates, blind blanks and standards results from the lab should be identified in the reporting of the samples. These data can be used to correct for bias or determine if the data should be eliminated from analyses.

Upon returning from the field, the data sondes will be checked against standards to determine the drift of the sensor over the sampling period. If drift on any sensor is outside of QC standards the data for that sensor may need to be removed from analysis. Regardless, the data sondes will be uploaded no later than the following day. The data files will be examined to determine if the upload was successful and no corruption of the files occurred. Once this is confirmed, a backup file will be made. The data sonde will then be cleared of memory, and battery levels checked.

General equipment maintenance tasks need to be completed at the end of the field sampling event. Post field logistics and tasks are described in SOP 8 (Post-Field Work Procedures and Equipment Maintenance). All gear and equipment will need to be rinsed and those pieces in need of repair or maintenance will be identified. A service schedule will be prepared so that gear is ready for the next field sampling. Maintenance required for the boat, boat trailer, and motor may be park-specific and observers will need to refer to the park specific or manufacturer documents. For more details, see SOP 8.

3.4 Permitting and Compliance

Various environmental permits and compliance procedures are required to implement this monitoring. As this protocol is implemented, we will proceed through project compliance as appropriate for each park according to federal as well as for state/commonwealth/territory guidelines. At present, under the National Environmental Policy Act (NEPA), we anticipate that this protocol falls under a Categorical Exclusion. Nevertheless, we will ensure full compliance with all existing and future regulations.

NPS, state, territorial, and commonwealth research permits will be obtained, in advance of any field activities, for each park where monitoring occurs (for further information see Appendix C). Permits will be evaluated on an annual basis, or other timeframe as stipulated in the permit itself. The research permit review process also includes NEPA compliance documentation, as discussed further below. The PI and Bio-tech will maintain all appropriate documentation. In NPSA Village permission should be obtained by personally contacting the village mayor to describe what the study is about, prior to initiating any work.

The compliance procedures as currently recommended by the PACN I&M Steering Committee will be followed. I&M will initiate compliance for this protocol in each park ensuring that each park's individual compliance method is followed. A Research Permit will be applied for in each park where monitoring will be conducted, and the park's compliance coordinator/specialist decides whether the Permit is adequate. If necessary an Environmental Screening Form will be filled out. Work will not begin in a park until the park-specific process has been followed, and the approval is signed off in appropriate forms.

4 - Data Handling, Analysis, and Reporting

Data handling, analysis, and reporting are treated as three interrelated steps in managing water quality monitoring information. Additional details and context for this chapter may be found in the PACN Data Management Plan (Dicus 2006) (online at http://www1.nature.nps.gov/im/units/pacn/data.cfm), which describes the overall information management strategy for the network. The PACN website (http://www1.nature.nps.gov/im/units/pacn/data.cfm) also contains guidance documents on various information management topics (e.g., report development, GIS applications, GPS use).

4.1 Project Information Management Overview

Project information management may be best understood as an ongoing or cyclic process, as shown in Figure 16. Specific yearly information management tasks for this project and their timing are described in Appendix L. Readers may also refer to each respective chapter section below for additional guidance and instructions.

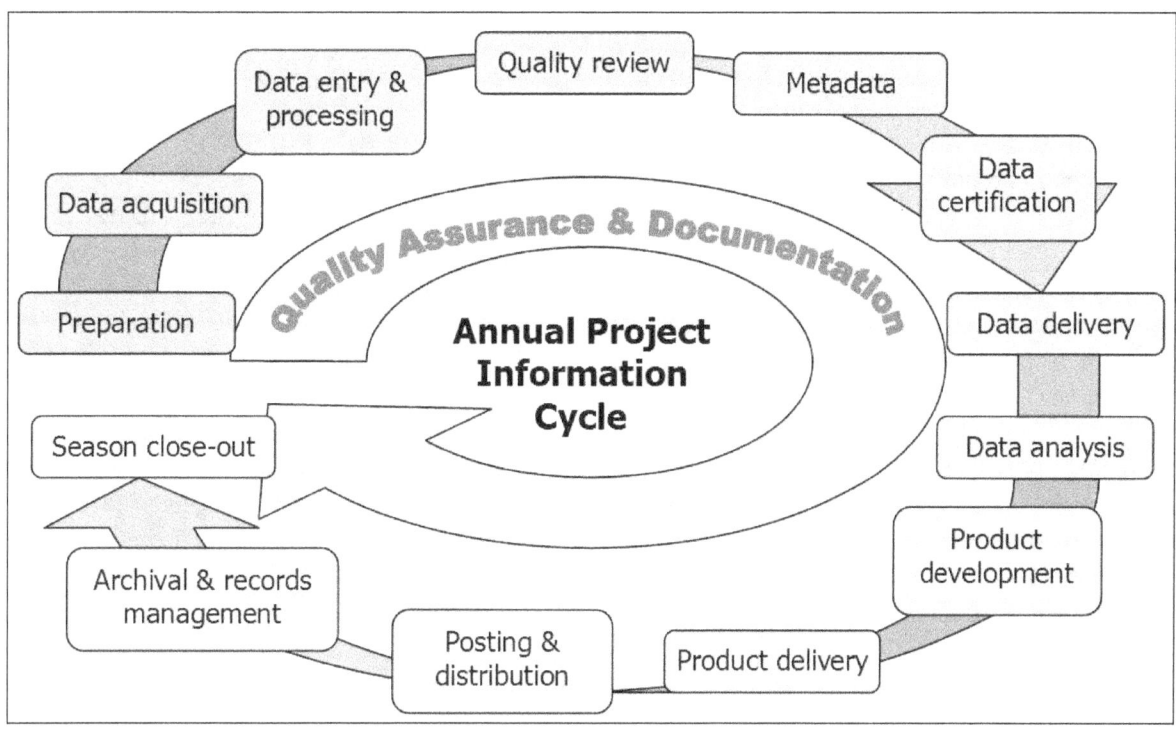

Figure 16. Idealized flow diagram of the cyclical stages of project information management, from pre-season preparation to season close-out. Note that quality assurance and documentation are thematic and not limited to any particular stage of the information life cycle.

The stages of this cycle are described in greater depth in later sections of this chapter, but can be briefly summarized as follows:

- Preparation: Training, logistics planning, print forms and maps
- Data acquisition: Field trips to acquire data

- Data entry & processing: Data entry and uploads into the working copy of the database, GPS data processing, etc.

- Quality review: Data are reviewed for quality and logical consistency

- Metadata: Documentation of the year's data collection and results of the quality review

- Data certification: Data are certified as complete for the period of record

- Data delivery: Certified data and metadata are delivered for archival and uploaded to the master project database

- Data analysis: Data are summarized and analyzed

- Product development: Reports, maps, and other products are developed

- Product delivery: Deliver reports and other products for posting and archival

- Posting & distribution: Distribute products as planned and/or post to NPS clearinghouses

- Archival and records management: Review analog and digital files for retention (or destruction) according to NPS Director's Order 19 (NPS 2001), online at http://data2.itc.nps.gov/npspolicy/DOrders.cfm).

- Retained files are renamed and stored as needed.

- Season close-out: Review and document needed improvements to project procedures or infrastructure, complete administrative reports, develop work plans for the coming season

4.2 Pre-season Preparations for Information Management

4.2.1 Set Up of Project Workspace
A section of the networked PACN server is reserved for this project, and access permissions are established so that project staff members have access to needed files within this workspace. Prior to each season, the Project Lead should make sure that network accounts are established for each new staff member, and that the Data Manager is notified to ensure access to the project workspace and databases. If network connections are too slow for efficient data entry and processing, individual staff members may set up a workspace on their own workstation, with periodic data transfer to the PACN server. Daily back ups of the workstation to an external hard drive will ensure that no data is lost. Additional details may be found in SOP 10 (Workspace Setup and Project Records Management).

4.2.2 GPS Loading and Preparation
The GIS Specialist and Project Lead should work together to ensure that target coordinates and data dictionaries are loaded into the GPS units prior to the onset of field work, and that GPS download software is available and ready for use. Additional details on GPS use and GPS data handling may be found in SOP 4 and on the PACN website.

4.2.3 Implementation of Working Database Copy

Prior to the field season, the Data Manager will implement a blank copy of the working database and ensure proper access on the part of the project staff. Refer to Overview for Database Design for additional information about the database design and implementation strategy.

4.3 Overview of Database Design

The PACN water quality database was created based on the NPSTORET desktop database application, but is modified and condensed to deal specifically with PACN water quality needs. NPSTORET is a Microsoft Access application designed around a series of templates that allow users to describe physical, chemical, and biological water quality monitoring activities in a format compatible with the EPA's STORET Import Module (SIM v.2). Templates exist for entering data about monitoring Projects, Stations, Metadata, and Results, and for producing Reports & Statistics.

PACN data management staff designed the PACN water quality database following the hierarchical data table organization of the Natural Resource Database Template (http://science.nature.nps.gov/im/apps/template/index.htm [last accessed 03July2006]; see the data dictionary and other documentation in Appendix M. The PACN data management staff is responsible for development and maintenance of the database, including customization of data summarization and export routines. The PACN water quality database has built in functionality for converting data into the correct format for importation into NPSTORET (for more information, see Appendix N. Water Quality Database User's Guide).

The database is divided into two components: one for entering, editing and error-checking data for the current season (i.e., the "working database copy"), and one that contains the complete set of certified data for the monitoring project (i.e., the "master project database"). A functional comparison of these two components is provided in Table 11.

Table 11. Functional comparison of the master project database and the working database.

Project Database Functions and Capabilities	Working Database	Master Database
Software platform for back-end data	MS Access	MS SQL Server or MS Access
Contains full list of sampling locations and taxa	X	X
Portable for remote data entry	X	
Forms for entering and editing current year data	X	
Quality assurance and data validation tools	X	X
Preliminary data summarization capabilities	X	
Full analysis, summarization and export tools		X
Pre-formatted report output		X
Contains certified data for all observation years		X
Limited editing capabilities, edits are logged		X
Full automated backups and transaction logging		X

Each of these components is based on an identical underlying data structure (tables, fields and relationships, as documented in Appendix M). The working database is implemented in Microsoft Access to permit greater flexibility when implementing on computers with limited or unreliable network access. Eventually, we would like to have the master database be implemented in Microsoft SQL Server in order to take advantage of the backup and transaction logging capabilities of this enterprise database software.

Both components have an associated front-end database application ("user interface" with forms and queries) implemented in Microsoft Access. The working database application has separate screens for data entry, data review, and quality validation tools. The master database application contains the analysis and summarization tools, including pre-formatted report output and exports to other software (e.g., for analysis and graphics production). This front-end application arrangement allows for modification and update of the user interface with no disruption to data entry continuity. The improved front-end file can be distributed to data entry staff, who link it to the back-end file, discard the out-dated front-end file, and proceed with their data entry work. Under this arrangement, data entry staff has no need to open the back-end file, thereby reducing the risk of improper deletions or other inadvertent data loss occurring within the protocol-specific data tables. In addition, a multi-user environment can be accommodated by storing the back-end file on a server available to all users via a computer network.

During the field season, each project crew will be provided with their own copy of a working database into which they enter, process, and quality-check data for the current season (refer to the section 4.4 in this report and to SOP 13. Data Entry and Verification). Once data for the field season have been certified they will be uploaded into the master database, which is then used to inform all reporting and analysis. This upload process is performed by the Data Manager, using a series of pre-built append queries.

4.4 Data Entry and Processing
The functional components for data entry into the working database are described in SOP 13. Each data entry form has built-in quality assurance components such as pick lists and validation rules to test for missing data or illogical combinations.

4.4.1 Regular Data Backups
Upon opening the working database, the user will be prompted to make a backup of the underlying data (see SOP 13). It is recommended that this be done on a regular basis, perhaps every day that new data are entered, to save time in case of mistakes or database file corruption. These periodic backup files should be compressed to save drive space, and may be deleted once enough subsequent backups are made. All such backups may be deleted after the data have passed the quality review and been certified.

4.4.2 Data Verification
Analyses performed to detect trends require data that are recorded properly and have acceptable precision and minimal bias. Poor quality data can limit detection of subtle changes in ecosystem patterns and processes, and may lead to incorrect conclusions. Quality assurance/quality control (QA/QC) procedures applied to ecological data include four procedural areas (or activities), ranging from simple to sophisticated, and inexpensive to costly:

- defining and enforcing standards for electronic formats, locally defined codes, measurement units, and metadata

- checking for unusual or unreasonable patterns in data

- checking for comparability of values between data sets

- assessing overall data quality

To the greatest extent possible, the water quality database application incorporates QA/QC strategies involving the first activity (defining and enforcing standards). The database design and the allowable value ranges assigned to individual fields within the data tables help to minimize the potential for data entry errors and/or the transcription of erroneously recorded data. The other activities are integrated in the validation phase (for more details, see section 4.5, Data Quality Review, and SOP 14. Data Quality Review and Certification).

4.4.3 Field Form Handling Procedures

As the field data forms are part of the permanent record for project data, they should be handled in a way that preserves their future interpretability and information content. To minimize the possibility of data loss, hardcopy data forms and field notebooks should be stored in a well organized fashion in a secure location, with photocopies or scanned data forms stored in a separate location (e.g., on the PACN data server). For more details, refer to SOP 11 (Field Form Handling Procedures).

4.4.4 Image Handling Procedures

Photographic images should also be handled and processed with care. For details on how to handle and manage these files, refer to SOP 12 (Managing Photographic Images).

4.4.5 GPS Data Procedures

The following general procedures should be followed for GPS data (see SOP 4 and Appendix L):

1. GPS data should be downloaded by the field crew from the units at the end of each field trip and stored in the project workspace (see SOP 10).

2. Raw files should be sent in a timely manner to the GIS Specialist for processing and correction.

3. The GIS Specialist will process the raw GPS data and store the processed data in the project workspace.

4. The GIS Specialist will upload corrected coordinate information into the database and create any GIS data sets.

The Field Lead should periodically review the processed GPS data to make sure that any problems are identified early on in the data collection process.

4.5 Data Quality Review

After the data have been entered and processed, they need to be reviewed by the Project Lead for quality, completeness, and logical consistency (see Data Certification and Delivery, and SOP 14).

61

4.5.1 Data Edits After Certification

Due to the high volume of data changes and/or corrections during data entry, it is not efficient to log all changes until after data are certified and uploaded into the master database. Prior to certification, daily backups of the working database provide a crude means of restoring data to the previous day's state. After certification, all data edits in the master database are tracked in an edit log (refer to Appendix M) so that future data users will be aware of changes made after certification. In case future users need to restore data to the certified version, we also retain a separate, read-only copy of the original, certified data for each year in the PACN Digital Library (refer to SOP 17).

4.5.2 Geospatial Data

The Project Lead and GIS Specialist may work together to review the surveyed coordinates and other geospatial data for accuracy. The purpose of this joint review is to make sure that geospatial data are complete and reasonably accurate, and also to determine which coordinates will be used for subsequent mapping and field work.

4.6 Metadata Procedures

Data documentation is a critical step toward ensuring that data sets are usable for their intended purposes well into the future. This involves the development of metadata, which can be defined as structured information about the content, quality, condition, and other characteristics of a given data set, both tabular and spatial. Additionally, metadata provide the means to catalog and search among data sets, thus making them available to a broad range of potential data users. Metadata for all PACN monitoring data will conform to Federal Geographic Data Committee (FGDC) guidelines and will contain all components of supporting information such that the data may be confidently manipulated, analyzed, and synthesized.

At the conclusion of the field season (according to the schedule in Appendix L), the Project Lead will be responsible for providing a completed, up-to-date metadata interview form to the Data Manager. The Data Manager and GIS Specialist will facilitate metadata development by consulting on the use of the metadata interview form, by creating and parsing metadata records from the information in the interview form, and by posting such records to national clearinghouses. For specific instructions, refer to SOP 15 (Metadata Development).

4.7 Data Certification and Delivery

Data certification is a benchmark in the project information management process that indicates that: 1) the data are complete for the period of record; 2) they have undergone and passed the quality assurance checks (Quality Review); and 3) that they are appropriately documented and in a condition for archiving, posting and distribution as appropriate. Certification is not intended to imply that the data are completely free of errors or inconsistencies which may or may not have been detected during quality assurance reviews.

To ensure that only quality data are included in reports and other project deliverables, the data certification step is an annual requirement for all tabular and spatial data. The Project Lead is primarily responsible for completing a PACN Project Data Certification Form, available on the PACN server and website. This brief form should be submitted with the certified data according to the timeline in Appendix L. For specific instructions, refer to SOPs 14 and 17.

4.8 Data Analysis

Note: Refer to Appendix L for the specific analysis tasks and their timing, and to SOP 19 (Data Analysis and Reporting) for a more detailed description of analytical procedures and for the complete schedule for project reports and other deliverables and the people responsible for them.

Data analysis addresses data validation issues and helps translate raw data into meaningful management information. Two initial steps for all water quality monitoring data have been identified: summarization and establishing range of variation. Ultimately, analyses of monitoring data are intended to detect change and assess resource status. These initial steps are encompassed in the larger construct of data management and data stewardship.

4.8.1 Analytical Approach

Four basic levels of analytical methods have been identified for our monitoring data: unit level, landscape level, trend assessment level, and synthesis (Table 12). The unit level addresses sample design questions regarding use of finite or infinite populations, and the establishment of relative, absolute, or index response variables. The landscape level identifies the spatial nature of sampling and the temporal allocation of samples, such as the revisit scheme in use. The trend assessment level integrates unit or landscape level data over time to detect change, where typically some form of regression is used to identify the slope or trend. Finally, synthesis examines patterns within and across vital signs and ecological and oceanographic factors to gain broad insight on ecological processes and integrity. Unit level, landscape level, and trend assessment level are addressed in this protocol. Synthesis will be addressed within and across multiple vital signs and is therefore left for future network consideration.

These analytical approaches will be applied to each of the water quality core parameters designated by this protocol.

Table 12. Approaches to analyzing water quality Vital signs data.

Level of Analysis	Description
Unit Level	Quality assurance and control routines and calculation of individual, site specific statistics from monitoring data
	Step 1 (Summarization): Measures of mean, median, variation, and other basic statistics. Include graphical presentation of data.
	Step 2 (Range of Variation): Establish historical or expected range of values, relation to regulatory levels, confidence estimates.
	Indices or other site-specific metrics may also be developed.
Landscape Level	Integration of unit level data across appropriate landscapes to address ecological status.
	Step 1: Integration of unit level summarization results across multiple locations and sites.
	Step 2: Integration of unit level variation results across multiple locations and sites. Additional refinement of spatial pattern analyses (e.g., cover, growth, and recruitment)
	Sample design, assumptions about the target population, actual data relationships, and evolving status determination methods will guide selection of appropriate methods.
Trend Assessment Level	Evaluation of Vital signs trends over time to detect change. Typically some form of regression will be among the methods used.
	Step 1: Integration of landscape level summarization over time.
	Step 2: Integration of landscape level variation results over time. Include establishing a direction and rate of change or variation that may be used to provide early warning. Confidence levels of documenting trend will be established.
	Parametric, nonparametric (design based) statistics, and models will be used. Trend assessment will also include accounting for influence from or correlating with drivers and stressors as feasible.

4.8.2 Status and Trend Analyses

The primary analytical strategies of interest to managers are anticipated to be status and long-term trends assessment (change detection). SOP 19 identifies the specific processes and methods used when preparing these analyses. The unit level analyses identified above are anticipated to be an initial step in the analytical process. This level is not typically completed in preparation for peer-review reporting except for programmatic and protocol evaluations and where unit level analyses provide insight to existing management concerns.

Additional analytical techniques may also be employed beyond those specified here or in SOP 19, as deemed necessary.

4.8.3 Analysis and Reporting Strategy

Standard Operating Procedure 19 identifies the processes and methods used for conducting analyses. The general process for all parameters not outlined below will follow the methods outlined by the USGS (Helsel and Hirsch 2002). These methods will not be written out here or in the SOPs as there is already an entire book dedicated to water-resource analyses and the authors feel redundancy is not necessary. However, simple analyses and those outside of the methods outlined in the Helsel and Hirsch (2002) are described below.

For all parameters, the first step will be to summarize measures of mean, median, and variance at each site using the replicates for chemical analyses and the stabilized sensor readings from the sonde. Non-detects and censored data will be used only in non-parametric analyses. These data will be used to calculate a site mean, median, and variance. This information will then be separated into two categories: fixed sites and random sites. Values will be compared to determine if there is a statistically significant different between the two categories. If there is no difference, the two categories will be grouped and analyzed together. If a difference exists, the following analyses will be done on both groups separately as appropriate (i.e. fixed will not be used for status). Status of the water resource for the park will be calculated by summarizing the mean, median, and variance of the data. Data will be described both annually and seasonally. This data will be compared to applicable water quality criteria standards and the differences noted. Any parameters exceeding the applicable water criteria standard will be highlighted. Those approaching (i.e. within 5%–10% of criteria value) will be noted.

Data from the extended deployment sonde will be used to normalize all physical parameters (this cannot be done for nutrient analyses). For example, DO changes throughout the day, so measurements at the beginning of the day are not comparable to measurements taken at midday. The differences between the extended deployment sonde and the point sample sonde will be compared, and the data then normalized to the first sampling period. Normalized data will then be imported into GIS for spatial analyses. Using the spatial analyst tool, the data for each parameter will be plotted and interpolated, using land mass masking, to give a graphical representation of parameter variance across the park unit as a whole. This is a graphical representation to aid management in identifying areas that would be potential target areas if there was management concern over an aquatic resource. It is intended for identification of potential management target areas only.

All data will be plotted (pH is log data and must be treated as such) with a regression around the points. Correlograms of raw data, data with seasonality removed, and seasonality and trend data removed along with 95 % confidence intervals will be plotted for reporting (McBride 2005). Fixed sites will be used to examine trend. Using the Sen slope estimator and the Seasonal Kendall trend test, fixed sites will be examined for changes to resource quality and the direction of change. Each season will be evaluated in addition to annual trend analyses. This data will be done on a park by park basis. Parks within Hawaii with similar resources will then be compared in similar fashion, followed by a PACN park wide analysis as applicable (i.e. marine components).

4.9 Reporting and Product Development

Clearly identified communication outlets are critical to producing positive results in resource protection and stewardship. Two briefing types have been identified: protected area managers' briefings and executive briefings (Table 13). The protected area managers' briefing provides a broad array of managers, scientists, and other parties with concise summary information. The Executive briefings will update superintendents and other VIPs on park-specific findings and employ non-technical language and graphics to explain potential resource issues. Both briefings are synthesis oriented and not intended to mirror a typical scientific presentation, but rather provide an opportunity to highlight key findings from the past year's work and identify potential management action items. These summary presentations will be accompanied by one to two page briefing statements that can also be used in preparation of the annual status and trends report for the network. To facilitate communication, annual timeframes are identified for each briefing type (Table 13, see also SOP 19).

The main audience for monitoring products and information is the resource managers and superintendents of each network park. Other NPS managers (not limited to resource staff), those in other protected areas, and appropriate partners will also be able to use the information when making management decisions. Other target audiences are also important, such as federal and state/territorial agencies, scientists, educators, and the general public. Inventory & Monitoring program managers are the typical audience for annual programmatic reporting and periodic protocol reviews.

Table 13. Schedule for recurring reporting to NPS management.

Briefing Type	Purpose	Primary Audience	Frequency
Protected area managers briefing	Communicate highlights and potential management action items, with 1–2 page briefing statements for each protocol	Park resource staff; Network staff; agency and academic scientists; other Federal, State, and Territorial Protected Area managers, discipline specialists, interpretive staff	Annually
Executive briefings (results synthesis)	Update Superintendents and other VIPs on park-specific findings and potential resource issues; suggest action items where appropriate	Individual Superintendents and other VIPs	As needed
Vital signs monitoring protocol report	Update park, regional, and national resource managers on network and park-specific findings and potential resource issues	Park resource managers, superintendents, regional ecologists, NPS Water Resources Division managers	Annually

4.9.1 Report Types

We anticipate that all reports generated in association with this vital sign will encompass the water quality core parameters identified in this protocol. Annual monitoring reports and park-based analyses for this vital sign will be prepared on a park-by-park basis, incorporating the network context as appropriate. A single annual vital signs monitoring protocol report will address monitoring results for all parks, treating each park individually. Abbreviated summaries of individual park results may also be prepared for park personnel (e.g., superintendent). At a three to five year interval, status and trend analysis will integrate data from multiple parks and re-assess monitoring strategies. This report will emphasize status and trend assessment over unit-level assessment. Within the status and trend report, the parks will be treated separately but will also include a network-wide synthesis.

The first status and trend report will be completed after three years of monitoring, and will focus on reassessing the monitoring protocol including methodology, study design, and statistical rigor. From this report, the protocol will be revised as necessary to meet the stated objectives. As needed, additional report summaries for individual parks, components of this vital sign, and analytical strategy may be generated from existing report material. Reporting is identified in SOP 19 by product type, purpose, targeted audience, responsible party, production frequency, and review process. This includes a cohesive suite of seven product categories: 1) program and protocol reviews, 2) monitoring protocol and project reports, 3) status and trends reports, 4) scientific writing and presentations, 5) management briefings, 6) website communication, and 7) interpretation and outreach.

Additional reporting, not explicitly identified here or in SOP 19, includes partnership efforts with other regional, national, and international programs. Examples include other regional status and trends reporting programs such as the biennial report to Congress or the USGS status and trends reports. This reporting will be handled by the PI on a case by case basis as time and resources permit.

4.9.2 Standard Report Format
Annual reports and trend analysis reports will use the NPS Natural Resource Publications templates, a pre-formatted Microsoft Word template document based on current NPS formatting standards. Annual reports will use the Natural Resource Report template, and trend analysis and other peer-reviewed technical reports will use the Natural Resource Technical Report template. These templates and documentation of the NPS publication standards are available at: http://www.nature.nps.gov/publications/NRPM/index.cfm.

4.9.3 Adaptive Management of Vital Signs Monitoring
The six monitoring goals of the PACN, identified in the PACN monitoring plan, focus on providing relevant, timely, and reliable monitoring data and information to park managers on resource condition and trends. A well-communicated monitoring program may enhance expectations for resource protection and stewardship, potentially fostering a stronger monitoring program and more effective resource management. Adaptive management requires this communication, as well as collaboration and coordination in fulfilling these efforts (Holling 1978; Walters 1986).

One facultative communication strategy emphasized in this PACN monitoring plan is prompt data analysis and communication on a regular schedule. This will ensure greater communication between field resource managers, scientists, data analysts, park interpretation staff, managers, and others. A clear communication strategy will also preclude both quality control and quality assurance issues that arise with delays in communication processes. Additionally, prompt and timely analysis, reporting, and communication of monitoring data and information are essential for adaptive management.

With these adaptive monitoring and management strategies and improved scientific understanding, revisions to the protocol will be required. Careful documentation of any changes to the protocol, and a library of previous protocol versions, are essential for maintaining consistency in data collection, and for appropriate treatment of the data during data summary and analysis. The steps for changing the protocol (either the protocol narrative or the SOPs) are outlined in SOP 20 (Revising the Protocol).

4.9.4 Review Products for Sensitive Information

Certain project information related to the specific locations of sensitive water bodies (i.e. water bodies not generally known to the public, but easily accessible and contaminated if known) may meet criteria for protection. In this case, the data should not be shared outside NPS except where a written confidentiality agreement is in place prior to data sharing. Before preparing data in any format for sharing outside NPS, including presentations, reports, and publications, the Project Lead should refer to the guidance in SOP 16 (Sensitive Information Procedures). Certain information that may convey specific locations of sensitive resources may need to be screened or redacted from public versions of products prior to release.

4.10 Product Delivery, Posting and Distribution

Refer to SOP 17 for the complete schedule for project deliverables and the people responsible for them and for detailed instructions on how to deliver final products. Upon delivery products will be posted to NPS websites and clearinghouses (e.g., NatureBib, NPSpecies, NPS Data Store) as appropriate (For more information, refer to SOP 18. Product Posting and Distribution).

4.10.1 STORET

The EPA has developed and maintained STORET as a database to house ambient water quality data collected by states, federal agencies, volunteer monitoring groups, and other entities. The Natural Resources Management Guideline (NPS-77) states that the NPS should provide water quality monitoring data to STORET as the national water quality repository. These archived data are then accessible to the public. Archiving PACN water quality data in STORET on an annual basis is a requirement in order to receive water quality vital signs funding from the Water Resources Division.

The NPS STORET database is maintained by the NPS Water Resources Division (WRD). To facilitate archiving NPS data in STORET the WRD has developed a series of Access-based templates (called NPSTORET), patterned after the Natural Resource Data Templates (http://science.nature.nps.gov/im/apps/template/), for Networks to use to enter their water quality data in a STORET-compatible format.

All water quality data collected by the PACN will be managed according to guidelines from the WRD. The PACN water quality database was created based on the NPSTORET desktop database application, but is modified and condensed to deal specifically to PACN water quality needs. PACN I&M data management staff will maintain a desktop copy of NPSTORET, which will be populated from the PACN water quality database annually after verification and validation of the dataset has occurred. PACN's NPSTORET contents will be transferred annually to NPS Water Resource Division for uploads to the STORET National Data Warehouse (Figure 17, Appendix L). Although WRD's data dissemination needs to dictate a monthly schedule for uploads to their data warehouse, PACN data collection and summation activities will be on an annual schedule requiring data uploads to the master WRD database only once a year.

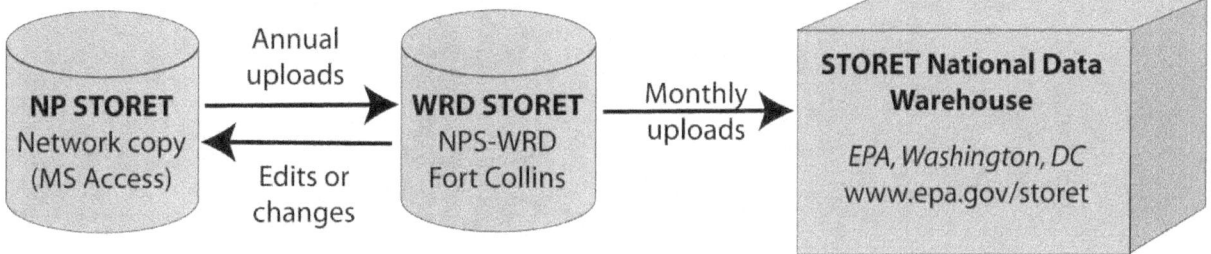

Figure 17. Data flow diagram for water quality data.

4.10.2 Holding Period for Project Data

To permit sufficient time for priority in publication, certified project data will be held upon delivery for a period not to exceed two years after it was originally collected. After the two year period has elapsed, all certified, non-sensitive data will be posted to the NPS Data Store. Note that this hold only applies to raw data, and not to metadata, reports or other products which are posted to NPS clearinghouses immediately after being received and processed.

4.10.3 Special Procedures for Sensitive Information

Products that have been identified upon submission by the Project Lead as containing sensitive information will either be revised into a form that does not disclose the locations of sensitive resources, or withheld from posting and distribution. When requests for distribution of the unedited version of products are initiated by the NPS, by another federal agency, or by another partner organization (e.g., a research scientist at a university), the unedited product (e.g., the full data set that includes protected information) may only be shared after a confidentiality agreement is established between NPS and the other organization. For more information, refer to SOP 16.

All official Freedom of Information Act (FOIA) requests will be handled according to NPS policy. The Project Lead will work with the Data Manager and the park FOIA representative(s) of the park(s) for which the request applies.

4.11 Archival and Records Management

All project files should be reviewed, cleaned up, and organized by the Project Lead on a regular basis (e.g., annually in January). Decisions on what to retain and what to destroy should be made following guidelines stipulated in NPS Director's Order 19, which provides a schedule indicating the amount of time that the various kinds of records should be retained (refer to SOP 10).

4.12 Season Close-out

After the conclusion of the field season, the Project Lead, Data Manager, and GIS Specialist should meet to discuss the recent field season, and to document any needed changes to the field sampling protocols, the working database application, or to any of the SOPs associated with the protocol. Refer to the section on Data Entry and Verification for additional close-out procedures not specifically related to project information management.

5 - Personnel Requirements and Training

5.1 Roles and Responsibilities

The water quality protocol will be implemented using a combination of existing in-park NPS staff, the PACN I&M Aquatic Ecologist, and a centralized, predominantly PACN-funded, technician for network level support, field work, and assistance (Table 14). This arrangement should effectively allow for monitoring in all PACN parks.

Appendix J to this protocol narrative identifies past and current names and contact information of personnel. See Appendix K for current individuals carrying out these tasks and Appendix L for specific yearly tasks for this project and their timing.

5.1.1 Project Lead (PL)

The PACN Aquatic Ecologist will serve as the PL and will be responsible for implementing this monitoring protocol in conjunction with the PACN Aquatic Biological Technician and park staff. The PACN Aquatic Ecologist will serve as the PACN I&M Program's lead point of contact. The PL will also serve as the primary point of contact to address problems and inquiries from the field. The PL will be responsible for overseeing data entry, data verification, data analysis, final report preparation and dissemination, and ensuring that data has been managed and archived appropriately. The PL works with the PACN Data Manager to ensure that the data management needs of this protocol are met, that data products are made available according to schedule, and that any required edits to archived data are documented according to network standards.

The PACN Aquatic Ecologist will also communicate budget, vital sign, and program needs with the PACN Program Manager. This position will be responsible for all I&M programmatic reporting as well as annual trend analysis and reporting, building upon park-based status reports. The PACN Aquatic Ecologist will coordinate periodic programmatic reviews of this Vital signs protocol to ensure the applicability of the protocols and data, and suggest and implement changes to the protocol design, the latter in cooperation with PL and Park Leads.

It is anticipated that the PL will either conduct or delegate each park's annual field program coordination, analysis, and reporting to the respective park's resource manager and/or designated ecologist(s). The PL will review each park's sampling effort and help ensure that operations and results meet the guidelines outlined in this protocol. The PL will supervise the centrally located Aquatic Biological Technician.

5.1.2 Park Lead

Ecologist or similar position with aquatic responsibilities, within a PACN Park.

The role of the Park Lead is to interact with the PL, assist PL with tracking schedules, park conflicts, and deadlines to help ensure all relevant park-based tasks are completed in a timely manner. The Park Lead will review reports and ensure that the Vital signs protocol objectives continue to meet park management needs.

Table 14. Roles and responsibilities for the PACN Water Quality Monitoring Protocol.

Role	Responsibilities
Project Lead	• Project oversight and administration • Track project objectives, budget, requirements, and progress toward project objectives • Facilitate communications between NPS and cooperator(s) • Coordinate and ratify changes to protocol • Assist in training field crews • Assist in performing data summaries and analysis, assist interpretation and report preparation • Review annual reports and other project deliverables for completeness and compliance with Inventory and Monitoring Program specifications • Maintain and archive project records • Upload certified data annually to NPSTORET • Project operations and implementation • Certify each season's data for quality and completeness • Complete reports, metadata, and other products according to schedule
Data Analyst	• Perform data summaries and analysis, assist interpretation and report preparation
Field Lead	• Train and ensure safety of field crew • Plan and execute field visits • Acquire and maintain field equipment • Oversee data collection and entry, verify accurate data transcription into database • Complete a field season report
Technicians	• Collect, record, enter and verify data
Data Manager	• Consultant on data management activities • Facilitate check-in, review and posting of data, metadata, reports, and other products to national databases and clearinghouses according to schedule • Maintain and update database application • Provide database training as needed
GIS Specialist	• Consultant on spatial data collection, GPS use, and spatial analysis techniques • Facilitate spatial data development and map output generation • Work with Project Lead and Data Analyst to analyze spatial data and develop metadata for spatial data products • Primary steward of GIS data and products
Program Manager	• Review annual reports for completeness and compliance with I&M standards and expectations
Park Biologists	• Facilitate logistics planning and coordination • Ensure project compliance with park requirements • Review reports, data and other project deliverables

5.1.3 Aquatic Biological Technician

The NPS-term Biological Technician, will be stationed in KAHO under the supervision of the PL located in HAVO.

This position will be 100% FTE. The Aquatic Biological Technician will be responsible for pre- and post- field season preparations and travel to parks to assist with and conduct on-site field monitoring as needed. The primary responsibilities will be logistical coordination, field data collection, data entry, data management, and equipment management. This individual will conduct some data analyses for annual reporting and participate in the preparation of preliminary reports. Water quality data will be downloaded and entered by the technician in the water quality database. This technician will work with the PL to merge all park databases into a final verified database. Initial preparation of analysis log files (see SOP 19) will be prepared under the direction of the PL. Assistance with report preparation will also be provided by the PL.

5.1.4 Park-based NPS Staff
Existing park-based resource staff will assist the PL and Aquatic Biological Technician with implementing field data collection. This cooperation will be important for remote parks (WAPA, AMME, NPSA). Park staff will accompany the field personnel for safety purposes and assist with field equipment. In some cases park staff will be trained to conduct and carry out monitoring when logistical constraints preclude the PACN Aquatic Ecologist or the Aquatic Biological Technician from conducting monitoring directly (i.e. AMME, WAPA, NPSA).

Park staff will also work with the PL and Park Lead to schedule field data collection.

5.1.5 PACN Data Manager
The Data Manager will provide guidance and, if appropriate, assistance with data management, archiving, adaptive database design, maintenance, data base integration, and data distribution. The PACN Data Manager will not be responsible for day-to-day activities required to implement this protocol, but will review the data and database-related practices of the PL and the Aquatic Biological Technician to ensure they meet programmatic and Vital signs standards and needs.

5.1.6 PACN GIS Specialist
The GIS Specialist will be responsible for the generation of individual park based sampling maps with geo-referenced sampling points provided by the PL. The PACN GIS Specialist will also be responsible for generating mapping locations and geo-referenced graphical representations of spatial analyses produced by the PL for associated water quality reporting.

5.1.7 PACN Program Manager
The PACN Program Manager will be responsible for general Aquatic program oversight. This includes periodic review of water quality reports, decisions regarding appropriations of I&M budget to the PACN aquatic monitoring programs, and the overall quality and performance of the PL in relation to the PACN aquatic program. The program manager is responsible for bringing any general monitoring issues beyond the scope of the PL responsibilities to the governing body of the PACN (PACN Board of Directors). The program manager is also responsible for making over-arching programmatic budgetary and staffing decisions affecting the PACN aquatic monitoring programs which the PL and Aquatic Biotech must then incorporate into planning efforts.

5.2 Qualifications and Training
All technical field staff will be trained in, and responsible for, familiarity with the information contained within SOPs, the protocol narrative, and the protocol database. Periodic training and recertification are required for maintaining motorboat operator certificates, and helicopter operations. These items are outlined in SOP 2, and involve a minimum of reading the full protocol (including narrative, SOP's, and appendixes), being trained by the PL to operate data

sondes, instruction in the proper completion of all data forms, and on site field implementation direction by the PL. Prior to the start of field sampling, all participating field personnel must refresh their methodological skills by reviewing SOP 2, and ensure their certifications are complete and up to date.

Each position requires minimum background knowledge, skills, and abilities. The PL position requires a graduate degree or equivalent experience in related discipline(s) (e.g., aquatic ecology, coral reef biology, oceanography, or other applicable biological/natural science field), experience in the field data collection, experience in statistics and data manipulation, and data management.

The Park Lead will typically be a park-based ecologist or resource manager, with experience and expertise that enables them to assist with all aspects of the program.

The Aquatic Biological Technician requires at minimum a bachelor's degree or equivalent experience in related discipline(s) (e.g., biological sciences, natural history, and oceanography). This position must be capable of underwater field operations, data collection, data management, post-processing, basic data analysis, and equipment maintenance.

The Data Manager requires experience in database management, records certification, SQL programming, and archiving. This position is hired through the PACN Program Manager and is responsible for the entire PACN data management program. The minimum qualification is a bachelors degree in computer science or related concentration, or other equivalent experience, plus experience with the afore mentioned skills.

The GIS specialist requires a bachelors degree in computer science or related concentration, plus specific experience with geo-referencing databases and programs. This position also requires experience in geographic information systems.

6 - Operational Requirements

This chapter outlines preparatory work necessary before monitoring occurs (pre-monitoring documents), annual workloads and field schedule, facility and equipment needs, start-up costs, and annual budgets.

6.1 Pre-Monitoring Documents
Requisite preparations for annual monitoring activities are summarized in SOP 1. At minimum, the PL, park lead, and aquatic biological technician should review all SOPs, the associated databases, and other products prior to initiating annual monitoring activities. As needed, the protocol narrative, appendices, SOPs, and databases shall be updated prior to initiating field-based monitoring efforts.

6.2 Annual Workload and Field Schedule
Field sampling will be conducted every three months in eight PACN parks. Scheduling sampling events on specific quarterly dates can be difficult due to inclement weather, personnel workloads, or other factors (e.g., typhoons, large waves in marine waters in the winter). In order to limit sources of variability, a one-week window will be used to plan when monitoring may occur at each park. Table 15 outlines a schedule of programmatic and monitoring related activities for this vital sign.

6.3 Facilities and Equipment
The Aquatic Biotech, Park Leads, and existing park-based staff will have all facility needs met by their respective host park or office, while equipment will be arranged through the PACN Aquatic Ecologist. Facility support, office space, and supply requirements for the Aquatic Biological Technician are outlined below.

Equipment and other supply needs are outlined in SOPs 1 and 5. Other than personal equipment for the Aquatic Biological Technician, items such as vehicles, boats, helicopter operations, scuba tanks and air, will be provided by the park where monitoring is occurring.

Office space and equipment needs for the Aquatic Biological Technician will be arranged by the PACN Aquatic Ecologist. Initially, these are to be provided at Kaloko Honokohau NHP. The office space and task-related equipment items include desk, chair, computer, software, digital camera, peripherals, and miscellaneous supplies along with occasional vehicle needs.

Park staff will be responsible for supplying laboratory space (i.e. for equipment calibration and nutrient analysis) and some long-term storage for monitoring supplies

Table 15. Annual (fiscal year) schedule of monitoring activity benchmarks, with responsible individual(s) identified

Month	Preparation & Maintenance	Responsible Party
Oct	Finalize budget for fiscal year. Begin equipment purchases	Park leads and PACN Aquatic Ecologist
Oct	Field Monitoring, plan monitoring for Jan	PL, Aquatic Biotech, and park staff
Nov	Field Monitoring, plan monitoring for Feb	PL, Aquatic Biotech, and park staff
Dec	Field Monitoring, plan monitoring for Mar	PL, Aquatic Biotech, and park staff
Jan	Field Monitoring, plan monitoring for Apr, Submit necessary IAP/IAGP's	PL, Aquatic Biotech, and park staff
Feb	Re-evaluate budget status for fiscal year	Park leads and PACN Aquatic Ecologist
Feb	Field Monitoring, plan monitoring for May	PL, Aquatic Biotech, and park staff
Mar	Mid-year equipment evaluation	Aquatic biotech and PACN Aquatic Ecologist
Mar	Field Monitoring, plan monitoring for Jun	PL, Aquatic Biotech, and park staff
Apr	Initial annual data analysis and report writing, write contracts/agreements necessary to continue work.	Park Leads, PACN Aquatic Ecologist, Aquatic Biotech
Apr	Field Monitoring, plan monitoring for Jul	PL, Aquatic Biotech, and park staff
May	Field Monitoring, plan monitoring for Aug	PL, Aquatic Biotech, and park staff
Jun	Field Monitoring, plan monitoring for Sep	PL, Aquatic Biotech, and park staff
Jul	Field Monitoring, plan monitoring for Oct	PL, Aquatic Biotech, and park staff
Aug	Field Monitoring, plan monitoring for Nov	PL, Aquatic Biotech, and park staff
Sep	Field Monitoring, plan monitoring for Dec	PL, Aquatic Biotech, and park staff
Sep	Close out year-end budget and finalize equipment purchases	PL and Aquatic Biotech
Sep	Complete annual reporting (protocol summary and annual analysis) may be completed earlier; this is the annual deadline for the previous year.	Park Leads, PACN Aquatic Ecologist, and Aquatic biotech
Sep	Field Monitoring, plan monitoring for Dec	PL and Aquatic Biotech
Sep	End of the year equipment evaluation	PL and Aquatic Biotech
Sep (or as needed)	Training/safety needs evaluation for PL, Aquatic Biological Technician, NPS Lead and park-based staff	PACN Aquatic Ecologist, PLCRP staff

6.4 Start-up Costs

Start-up costs are identified separately from annual, implemented monitoring, and maintenance expenses. In general, start-up costs are anticipated to be somewhat substantial, as monitoring of this vital sign builds upon limited existing park capacities and resource management personnel. It is not feasible to incorporate all start-up costs into a single fiscal year because a substantial amount of the cost is in the monitoring equipment (approximately $35,000 per park to have all parks with their own equipment), so a phase-in plan will be used with this protocol. Some equipment will be centrally located with I&M and moved between parks by the Aquatic Biological Technician or Aquatic Ecologist when monitoring takes place. This is quite feasible with the Hawaii parks; however WAPA and NPSA will need to have equipment provided to them. Also, annually recurring fixed costs include equipment maintenance, salaries, training, certification, and travel-related expenses.

Approximately $3,500 per park is anticipated for purchasing field monitoring supplies (nutrient analysis sample bottles, filters, cleaning supplies, and calibration chemicals). These supplies will be provided using existing appropriated funds from the I&M program as long as funds are available.

For the Aquatic Biological Technician, approximately $13,000 in start-up expenses are anticipated to provide dive gear, training, computer equipment, office material, and recruitment costs (Table 16). These start-up costs assume existing office space as well as durable and consumable supplies are already in place.

Implementation of this vital signs monitoring program will largely be the responsibility of PACN I&M and NPS staff with some assistance from parks and cooperators when needed, particularly in those parks that are somewhat remote (i.e. WAPA, NPSA, AMME).

Table 16. Start-up PACN costs for the aquatic biological technician.

Start-up costs	PACN
Dive equipment	$2,500
Training and certification	$2,000
Computer and software	$3,500
Desk and office supplies	$2,000
Position rating and recruitment	$3,000
Total	$13,000

6.5 Annual Budget

Annual expense estimates (based on best practices) for the water quality vital signs monitoring program are outlined in Table 17. These expenses are based on monthly sampling in each park, using the Aquatic Biological Technician and the Aquatic Ecologist for primary field work, and existing park-based staff for all additional field work (approximately 2 additional days per month when necessary). As this protocol, sample design, field visit schedule, and safety and other considerations evolve, this budget will need refining. In addition, these estimates are based on 2007/2008 expenses.

These expenses are dedicated for implementation of this monitoring protocol, and are outlined in detail. These include salary (with COLA and benefits), travel, computer and office supplies, office space, personal equipment, and mandatory training and certification expenses related to maintaining dive certification. Most of the Aquatic Biological Technician's time is anticipated to be devoted to this vital sign, and the salary amounts in Table 17 reflect this. Personnel salaries were assumed to be GS-7, step 5, 100% FTE, 2007 pay schedule with 25% COLA and 25% benefits for the following personnel: Aquatic Biological Technician and other technicians. Personnel salaries were assumed to be GS-11, step 5, 25% FTE, 2007 pay schedule with 25% COLA and 25% benefits for the following personnel: Aquatic Ecologist, Data Manager, and the GIS Specialist. The Program manager was assumed to be GS-13, step 1, 4% FTE, 2007 pay schedule with 25% COLA and 25% benefits. Not included in the table, and in addition, other park based support personnel costs were estimated to be GS-7, Step 5, for 6 pay periods/year [25% FTE] with 25% COLA, 25% hazard and 25% benefits) per park ($39,000 / year).

For the PL and park-based staff; existing funds will be used to support these individuals' personnel costs and associated supplies, travel, and training expenses. The expenses directly related to this protocol are identified in Table 17. This includes all costs associated with boat use and scuba supplies, as well as field monitoring equipment. It is the responsibility of the PACN Aquatic Ecologist with assistance from park staff and the Aquatic Biological Technician, to ensure that all appropriate compliance and permitting has been completed prior to the start of any fieldwork.

Table 17. Annual itemized expenses for the Water Quality monitoring protocol by park.

2008 Water Quality Protocol Budget Estimates											
Parks	ALKA	AMME	HALE	HAVO	KAHO	KALA	NPSA	PUHE	PUHO	USAR	WAPA
Salaries											
Aquatic Ecologist	$ 1,344	$ 1,920	$ 3,264	$ 768	$ 2,112	$ 3,264	$ 4,800	$ 1,344	$ 1,344	$ 288	$ 3,264
Aquatic Biotech	$ 1,200	$ 1,200	$ 2,400	$ 600	$ 1,680	$ 1,800	$ 2,400	$ 1,200	$ 1,200	$ 240	$ 1,800
Data Manager	$ 192	$ 384	$ 384	$ 96	$ 384	$ 384	$ 384	$ 192	$ 192	$ -	$ 384
Gis Specialist	$ 100	$ 100	$ 400	$ 100	$ 400	$ 400	$ 400	$ -	$ -	$ -	$ 400
Program Manager	$ 132	$ 132	$ 528	$ 132	$ 264	$ 264	$ 264	$ 132	$ 132	$ 132	$ 264
Technicians	$ -	$ 720	$ -	$ -	$ 240	$ 600	$ 1,200	$ -	$ -	$ -	$ 600
Sub-Total	*$ 2,968*	*$ 4,456*	*$ 6,976*	*$ 1,696*	*$ 5,080*	*$ 6,712*	*$ 9,448*	*$ 2,868*	*$ 2,868*	*$ 660*	*$ 6,712*
Travel											
Camping Cost	$ -	$ -	$ 500 00	$ 75 00	$ -	$ 500 00	$ 400 00	$ -	$ -	$ -	$ -
Hotel Cost	$ -	$ 600	$ -	$ -	$ -	$ -	$ 400	$ -	$ -	$ -	$ 500
Airfare Cost	$ -	$ 1,200	$ 1,600	$ -	$ -	$ 1,600	$ 2,560	$ -	$ -	$ -	$ 2,000
Vehicle Cost	$ 400	$ 800	$ 900	$ -	$ 400	$ -	$ -	$ 400	$ 400	$ -	$ 500
Sub-Total	*$ 400*	*$ 2,600*	*$ 3,000*	*$ 75*	*$ 400*	*$ 2,100*	*$ 3,360*	*$ 400*	*$ 400*	*$ -*	*$ 3,000*
Equipment & Supplies											
Calibrations	$ 232 49	$ 232 49	$ 232 49	$ 232 49	$ 232 49	$ 232 49	$ 232 49	$ 232 49	$ 232 49	$ 232 49	$ 232 49
Analysis	$ 2,080	$ 2,080	$ 2,080	$ 520	$ 4,160	$ 4,160	$ 4,160	$ 780	$ 2,080	$ -	$ 4,160
Sub-Total	*$ 2,312*	*$ 2,312*	*$ 2,312*	*$ 752*	*$ 4,392*	*$ 4,392*	*$ 4,392*	*$ 1,012*	*$ 2,312*	*$ 232*	*$ 4,392*
Other											
Training & certs	$ 100	$ 100	$ 100	$ 100	$ 100	$ 100	$ 100	$ 100	$ 100	$ 100	$ 100
Office necessities	$ 100	$ 100	$ 100	$ 100	$ 100	$ 100	$ 100	$ 100	$ 100	$ 100	$ 100
Sub-Total	*$ 200*	*$ 200*	*$ 200*	*$ 200*	*$ 200*	*$ 200*	*$ 200*	*$ 200*	*$ 200*	*$ 200*	*$ 200*
Totals	*$ 5,880*	*$ 9,568*	*$ 12,488*	*$ 2,723*	*$ 10,072*	*$ 13,404*	*$ 17,400*	*$ 4,480*	*$ 5,780*	*$ 1,092*	*$ 14,304*
Grand Total $97,196											

Costs associated with existing park-based staff are incorporated, as these positions already exist with assigned duties not related to this vital sign. Should this collaboration not be available, additional expenses should be expected. Additional partnerships and collaborators will be pursued regardless, to further the mission of NPS, the I&M program, Parks, and partners and collaborators. This protocol was specifically written as a minimum for what the PACN could accomplish given the current personnel staffing and budget. It is expected that PACN personnel will search out other partnerships through agreements and collaboration to expand this monitoring effort. However, what is presented in this protocol should be able to be accomplished regardless of collaborative efforts. Nevertheless, budget cuts do happen. If this were the case, the tracking of status and trends would be inhibited. It would mean missing data and longer time periods to detect trends. A significant reduction in effort would be available requiring more input from the parks for the program to continue. As with any monitoring program if cuts are deep enough the program would end.

7 - Literature Cited

American Samoa Environmental Protection Agency. 2005. Water quality standards. American Samoa Environmental Protection Agency. Pago Pago, American Samoa. Online. (http://asepa.gov/water-quality.asp). Accessed 11 November 2010.

Anthony, S. S., C. D. Hunt, Jr., A. M. D. Brasher, L. D. Miller, and M. S. Tomlinson. 2004. Water quality on the island of Oahu, Hawaii, 1999–2001: U.S. Geological Survey Circular 1239, 41 p. U. S. Geological Survey. Denver, Colorado.

Beard, G. R., W. A. Scott, and J. K. Adamson. 1999. The value of consistent methodology in long-term environmental monitoring. Environmental Monitoring and Assessment 54:239–258.

Betancourt, W. Q., and R. S. Fujioka. 2009. Evaluation of enterococcal surface protein genes as markers of sewage contamination in tropical recreational waters. Water Science & Technology 60: 261-266

Betancourt, W. Q., and R. S. Fujioka. 2005. Bacteroides Spp. as reliable marker of sewage contamination in Hawaii's environmental waters using molecular techniques. Water Science & Technology 54: 101-107

Betts, R. A. 2004. Global vegetation and climate: Self-beneficial effects, climate forcings and climate feedbacks. Journal of Physics IV France. 121:37–60.

Beyers, D. W., J. A. Rice, W. H. Clements, and C. J. Henry. 1999. Estimating physiological cost of chemical exposure: integrating energetics and stress to quantify toxic effects in fish. Canadian Journal of Fisheries Aquatic Science 56(5): 814–822.

Bienfang, Paul 2006. Assess nutrient flux sources and water quality of ponds within Kaloko-Honokohau National Historic Park. Hawaii-Pacific Islands Cooperative Ecosystems Studies Unit Report. Task Agreement CA8052-AO-001. Pp.1–48. University of Hawaii. Honolulu, Hawaii.

Brown, B. E. 1997. Coral bleaching: causes and consequences. Coral Reefs. 16:S129–S138.

Brown, V. 2003. Causes for concern: Chemicals and wildlife. World Wildlife Fund DetoX Campaign. Brussels, Belgium. Online. (http://assets.panda.org/downloads/causesforconcern.pdf). Accessed 29 October 2009.

Commonwealth of the Northern Mariana Islands Department of Environmental Quality. 2004. Water Quality Standards. 43 pp. Commonwealth of the Northern Mariana Islands Department of Environmental Quality. Garapan, Saipan. (http://www.deq.gov.mp/artdoc/Sec9art52ID133.pdf). Accessed 15 November 2010.

Connell, J. H., T. P. Hughes, and C. C. Wallace. 1997. A 30-year study of coral abundance, recruitment, and disturbance at several scales in space and time. Ecological Monographs 67: 461–488.

Cosser, P. R. 1997. editor. Nutrients in marine and estuarine environments, State of the Environment Technical Paper Series (Estuaries and the Sea), Department of the Environment, Canberra, Australia.

Craig, P., and L. Basch. 2001. Developing a coral reef monitoring program for the National Park of American Samoa. National Park of American Samoa. Pago Pago, American Samoa. (http://www.botany.hawaii.edu/basch/uhnpscesu/pdfs/sam/Craig2001DevAS.pdf). Accessed 15 November 2010.

Croze, H. 1982. Monitoring within and outside protected areas. Pages 628–633 *in* J. A. McNeely and K. R. Miller, editors. National parks, conservation and development: The role of protected areas in sustaining society. Proceedings of the World Congress on National Parks, October 11–22, 1982, Bali, Indonesia. Smithsonian Institution Press, Washington, D.C.

Davis, G. E. 1989. Design of a long-term ecological monitoring program for Channel Islands National Park, California. Natural Areas Journal 9:80–89.

DeBacker, M. D., C. C. Young (editor), P. Adams, L. Morrison, D. Peitz, G. A. Rowell, M. Williams, and D. Bowles. 2005. Heartland Inventory and Monitoring Network and Prairie Cluster Prototype Monitoring Program Vital Signs Monitoring Plan. National Park Service, Heartland Inventory and Monitoring Network and Prairie Cluster Prototype Monitoring Program, Wilson's Creek National Battlefield, Republic, Missouri, USA. 104 p. plus appendices.

De Carlo, E. H., V. L. Beltran, M. S. Tomlinson, K. J. Spencer, and J. E. Hubert. 2001. Trace elements in the aquatic environment of Hawaii: Effects of urbanization. American Chemical Society National Meeting. April 1 – 5, 2001. San Diego, California.

Quinn, J. F., and C. van Riper, III. 1990. Design considerations for national park inventory databases. Pages 5–14 *in* C. van Riper, III, T. J. Stohlgren, S. D. Veirs, Jr., and S. C. Hillyer, editors. Examples of resource inventory and monitoring in National Parks of California. Proceedings of the Third Biennial Conference on Research in California's National Parks, September 13–15, 1990, University of California, Davis, California.

DeVerse, K. and E. DiDonato. 2006. Appendix I: Water quality report. *In* L. HaySmith, F. L. Klasner, S. H. Stephens, and G. H. Dicus. Pacific Island Network Vital Signs Monitoring Plan: Phase III (draft) report. National Park Service, Pacific Island Network, Hawaii National Park, Hawaii.

Dicus, G. H. 2006. Data management plan for the Pacific Island Network. National Park Service, Pacific Island Network, Hawaii National Park, Hawaii.

Ehrlich, P. R. 1991. Foreward: Facing up to climate change. Pages ix–xiii *in* Global climate change and life on earth. Chapman, and Hall, Inc. Boca Raton, Florida.

Fabricius, K. E. 2005. Effects of terrestrial runoff on the ecology of corals and coral reefs: review and synthesis. Marine Pollution Bulletin 50:125–146.

Fujioka, R. S., G. K. Rijal, and J. A. Bonilla. 1998. An innovative approach to assess and monitor the quality of coastal water. Project Completion Report: WRRC-98-13 Water Resources Research Center, University of Hawaii at Manoa, Honolulu, Hawaii. Prepared for Sea Grant College Program, University of Hawaii. Honolulu, Hawaii.

Garrison, G. H., C. R. Glenn, and G. M. McMurty. 2004. Measurement of submarine groundwater discharge in Kahana Bay, Oʻahu, Hawaiʻi. Limnology and Oceanography 48:920–928.

Glenn, E. P., C. M. Smith, and M. S. Doty. 1990. Influence of antecedent water temperatures on standing crop of a *Sargassum* spp.-dominated reef flat in Hawaii. Marine Biology 105: 323–328.

Green, R. H., and S. R. Smith. 1997. Sample program design and environmental impact assessment on coral reefs. Pages 1459–1464 *in* Proceedings of the 8th International Coral Reef Symposium. June 24 – 29, 1996. Panama City, Panama.

Gross, J. E. 2003. Developing conceptual ecological models for monitoring programs. National Park Service, Fort Collins, Colorado.

Guam Environmental Protection Agency. 2001. Revised Guam Water Quality Standards. Public Law 26-32. 122 pp.

Hayes, J. T. 1991. Global climate change and water resources. Pages 18 – 42 *in* Global climate change and life on earth. pp. 18–42. Chapman, and Hall, Inc. Boca Raton, Florida.

HaySmith, L., F. L. Klasner, S. H. Stephens, and G. H. Dicus. 2005. Pacific Island Network Vital Signs monitoring plan. Natural Resource Report NPS/PACN/NRR—2006/003. National Park Service, Fort Collins, Colorado. Online (http://www1.nature.nps.gov /im/units/pacn/monitoring/plan.cfm). Accessed 1 March 2007.

Helsel D. R., and R. M. Hirsch. 2002. Statistical methods in water resources. Pages 65–95 *in* Techniques of water-resources investigations of the United States Geological Survey. Book 4, Hydrologic analysis and interpretation. U.S. Geological Survey, Washington, D.C. Online. (http://water.usgs.gov/pubs/twri/twri4a3/). Accessed 19 October 2009.

Hodgkiss, I. J., and K. C. Ho. 1997. Are changes in N:P ratios in coastal waters the key to increased red tide blooms? Hydrobiologia 352 (1–3):141–147.

Hoegh-Guldberg, O. 1999. Climate change, coral bleaching and the future of the world's coral reefs. Marine and Freshwater Research 50:839–866.

Holling, C. S. 1978. Adaptive environmental assessment and management. John Wiley and Sons, London.

Houk, P. 2001. State of the reef report for Saipan Island, Commonwealth of the Northern Mariana Islands. Saipan, MP, Division of Environmental Quality. 59 pp.

Hughes T. P. 1994. Catastrophes, phase shifts, and large-scale degradation of a Caribbean coral reef. Science 265: 1547–1551.

Irwin, R. J. 2004. Part B Lite QA/QC Checklist for Aquatic Vital Signs Monitoring Protocols and SOPs. National Park Service, Water Resources Division, Fort Collins, Colorado Online. (http://www.nature.nps.gov/water/Vital_Signs_Guidance/Guidance_Documents/PartBLite.pdf). Accessed 15 November 2010.

Jameson S. C., M. V. Erdmann, J. R. Karr, G. R. Gibson Jr., and K. W. Potts. 2001. Charting a course toward diagnostic monitoring: A continuing review of coral reef attributes and a research strategy for creating coral reef indexes of biotic integrity. Bulletin of Marine Science 69(2):701–744.

Jones, K. B. 1986. The inventory and monitoring process. Pages 1–9 in A. Y. Cooperrider, R. J. Boyd, and H. R. Steward, editors. Inventory and monitoring of wildlife habitat. USDI Bureau of Land Management Service Center. Denver, Colorado.

Lapointe, B. E., J. D. O'Connell, and G. S. Garrett. 1990. Nutrient couplings between on-site sewage disposal systems, groundwaters, and nearshore surface waters of the Florida Keys. Biogeochemistry 10:289–307.

Leatherman, S. P. 1991. Impact of climate-induced sea level rise on coastal areas. Pages 170-179 in Global climate change and life on earth. Chapman, and Hall, Inc. Boca Raton, Florida.

Li, Y. H. 1988. Denudation rates of the Hawaiian Islands by rivers and groundwaters. Pacific Science 42:253–266.

Long, E. R., D. D. MacDonald, S. L. Smith, and F. D. Calder. 1995. Incidence of adverse biological effects within ranges of chemical concentrations in marine and estuarine sediments. Environmental Management 19(1):81–97.

Matson, E. 1986. Terrigenous material in coastal sediments of Guam and Saipan. Technical Report No. 73. Water and Environmental Research Institute, University of Guam. 33 pp.

McDonald, T. L. 2003. Environmental trend detection: A review. Environmental Monitoring and Assessment 85:277–292.

National Park Service (NPS). 1916. National Park Service Organic Act. (16 U.S.C. §§ 1 et seq.) Online. (http://www.nps.gov/legacy/organic-act.htm). Accessed 15 November 2010.

National Park Service (NPS). 2006. Management policies, 2001. Department of Interior, National Park Service, Washington, D.C. 180 pp. Online. (http://data2.itc.nps.gov/npspolicy/index.cfm) Accessed 15 November 2010.

National Park Service (NPS). 2001. Director's order 19: Records management. U.S. Department of the Interior, National Park Service, Washington, D.C. Online. (http://www.nps.gov/policy/DOrders/DOrder19.html61). Accessed December 10, 2009.

National Park Service (NPS). 2006. Vital Signs Monitoring, Program Goals, Purpose and Definitions. National Park Service, Fort Collins, Colorado Online. (http://science.nature.nps.gov/im/monitor/ProgramGoals.cfm). Accessed 8 June 2006.

National Park Service (NPS) Pacific Island I&M Network. Proceedings of a planning meeting for water quality monitoring, Kailua-Kona, Hawaii. 12–13 August 2003.

Quinn, J. F., and C. van Riper, III. 1990. Design considerations for national park inventory databases. Pages 5–14 in C. van Riper, III, T. J. Stohlgren, S. D. Veirs, Jr., and S. C. Hillyer, editors. Examples of resource inventory and monitoring in National Parks of California. Proceedings of the Third Biennial Conference on Research in California's National Parks, September 13–15, 1990, University of California, Davis, California.

Richardson, L. L. 1998. Coral disease: What is really known? TREE. 12:438–443.

Rocke, T. E., and M. D. Samuel. 1999. Water and sediment characteristics associated with avian botulism outbreaks in wetlands. Journal of Wildlife Management. 63(4):1249–1260.

Roman, C., R. Irwin, R. Curry, M. Kolipinski, J. Portnoy, L. Cameron. 2003. White-Paper Report of the Park Service Vital Signs Workgroup for Monitoring Marine and Estuarine Environments. Workgroup Convened April 3–4, 2002, North Atlantic Coast CESU at the University of Rhode Island, Narragansett, Rhode Island, 20pp.

Rowell, G. A., M. H. Williams, and M. D. DeBacker. 2005. Data Management Plan: Heartland I&M Network and Prairie Cluster Prototype Monitoring Program. Heartland I&M Network and Prairie Cluster Prototype Monitoring Program Wilson's Creek National Battlefield, Republic, Missouri.

Salati, E., and C. A. Nobre. 1991. Possible climatic impacts of tropical deforestation. Climatic Change. 19(1–2):177–196.

Sedwick, P. N., G. M. McMurty, and G. W. Tribble. 1990. Chemical alteration of seawater by lava from Kilauea Volcano, Hawaii. Marine Geology, 96(1991)151–158.

Skalski, J. R. 1990. A design for long-term status and trends monitoring. Journal Environmental Management 30:139–144.

Skalski, J. R. 2005. Long-term monitoring: Basic study designs, estimators, and precision and power calculations. Report submitted to NPS PACN Inventory and Monitoring Program.

Smith, J. E., C. M. Smith, and C. L. Hunter. 2001. An experimental analysis of the effects of herbivory and nutrient enrichment on the benthic community composition of a Hawaiian reef. Coral Reefs 19:332–342.

Sutherland, K. P., J. W. Porter, and C. Torres. 2004. Disease and immunity in Caribbean and Indo-Pacific zooxanthellate corals. Marine Ecology Progressive Series 266:273–302.

State of Hawaii Department of Health. 2004. Water quality standards. HAR Title 11, Ch. 54. 62 pp.

United States Geological Survey Water Resources Division (USGS-WRD). 2003. USGS plan for water-resources science in the Pacific Islands Region. Science Plan. Honolulu, Hawaii

Valiela, I., J. Costa, K. Foreman, J. M. Teal, B. Howes, and D. Aubrey. 1990. Transport of groundwater-bourne nutrients and their effects on coastal water. Biogeochemistry 10:177–197.

Valiela, I. 1995. Marine Ecological Processes. Second edition. Springer-Verlag New York, Inc. NewYork, New York. 686 pp.

Walters, C. J. 1986. Adaptive management of renewable resources. Macmillan Publishing Company, New York, New York.

Wetherald, R. T. 1991. Changes of Temperture and Hydrology Caused by an Increase of Atmospheric Carbon Dioxide as Predicted by General Circulation Models. Pages 1 - 17 in Global climate change and life on earth. Chapman, and Hall, Inc. Boca Raton, Florida.

White, P. S., and S. P. Bratton. 1980. After preservation: The philosophical and practical problems of change. Biological Conservation 18:241–255.

Wiersma, G. B. 1984. Integrated global background monitoring network. Paper presented at Symposium: Research and Monitoring in Circumpolar Biosphere Reserves Symposium. Waterton Biosphere Reserve, 27–31 August, Waterton Lakes, Alberta, Canada.

Wolanski, E., R. H. Richmond, G. Davis, and V. Bonito. 2003. Water and fine sediment dynamics in transient river plumes in a small, reef-fringed bay, Guam. Estuarine and Coastal Shelf Science. 56: 1029–1043.

NPS 988/108127, June 2011